JESUS BRINGS GOD'S M...

GREAT WORSHIP FOR KIDS

Middler/Junior

STANDARD PUBLISHING
Cincinnati, Ohio

Session Writers

Vicki Ziese, Sessions 1-5

Debra Orr, Sessions 6-9

Anna Hennig, Sessions 10-13

Activity Pages

Dawn Korth

Andrew Quach

Scripture quotations marked NIV are from the HOLY BIBLE—NEW INTERNATIONAL VERSION, Copyright © 1973, 1978, 1984 International Bible Society. Used by permission of Zondervan Bible Publishers.

Scriptures marked ICB quoted from the International Children's Bible, New Century Version, copyright © 1986, 1988 by Word Publishing, Dallas, Texas 75039. Used by permission.

The Standard Publishing Company, Cincinnati, Ohio
A division of Standex International Corporation
©1994 by The Standard Publishing Company

All rights reserved.
Printed in the United States of America

ISBN 0-7847-0018-4

Jesus Brings God's Message

Unit One: Trust God Who Keeps His Promises

1. A Promise Is Kept — 9
   You Can Depend on It! 13 • God Promised, 14 • Promises to Me! 15
2. The Savior Is Coming — 16
   Jesus, 20 • What's Ahead? God Knows the Future, 21 • Don't Fear the Future, 22
3. A Message to Israel — 23
   Number 9, 27 • A Promise Is a Promese, 28
4. The Savior Is Here — 29
   Songs and Scriptures, 33 • Jesus Is a Special Gift, 34 • Giving Myself to God, 35
5. An Escape to Egypt — 36
   God Will Protect, 40 • The Key 15, 41 • Write a Story, 42

Unit Two: God Answers When We Pray

6. The Wise One — 43
   How's Your Vision? 47 • Words of Wisdom, 48
7. God's Great Forgiveness — 49
   God's Great Forgiveness, 53 • Mystery Verse, 54 • If and Then, 55
8. Obeying God — 56
   God Knows Our Hearts and Minds, 60 • Make a Parable Book/Promises for Those Who Obey, 61 • Are You Obeying? 62
9. Overcoming Temptation — 63
   Super Victory, 67 • Protected by Armor, 68 • Excercise Time, 69

Unit Three: Jesus Teaches About Happiness

10. Worthy to Be Followed — 70
    Jeb, the Gold Prospector, 74 • Say Cheese! 75 • God Is Worthy, 76
11. I've Got the Joy Down in My Heart — 77
    Hearts of Joy, 81 • Joy for All Occasions, 82 • The Heart of It All, 83
12. More Important Than Anything — 84
    Action Packed Game, 88 • Photos for an Album, 89 • Write the News, 90
13. For Eternity — 91
    Match the Shape, 95 • A Lesson in Construction, 96

Is Your Worship Great?

It doesn't seem great to me . . .

What do you mean?

Great worship . . . Our Middler/Junior worship is hardly what you'd call great.

Why is that?

Well, I guess everyone has a different idea of what our worship time should be. Our Bible school superintendent calls it "extended session," and wants us to have a second Sunday school hour. But Sunday school is designed for instruction. Our worship time is for worshiping God.

That makes sense to me. What do the parents think?

Some of them want us to have a carbon copy of an adult worship service—including a sermon.

Uh-oh. That's not realistic for many Middlers and Juniors, is it?

In my experience it's not. Kids that age don't think like adults, respond like adults—and they certainly don't sit still as long as adults! I want them to worship God in ways that are appropriate for their level of development.

Absolutely. And you're not just keeping them occupied while their parents are in worship, as some people believe. The children's worship is as important and meaningful as the parents'.

Yes. I want every kid there to know God personally and to respond to Him in praise and thanksgiving. I want the kids to learn that worship is active, not passive. It's something they themselves do— not just the leader in front of the group.

Sounds to me as if you're right on target. What makes your Middler/Junior worship less than great?

It's hard to involve all the pupils sometimes. There are older kids and younger kids. Some are quick and bright, and some work more slowly and need more encouragement. Some are more comfortable in small groups than others. It's hard to appeal to all their differences.

The writers of *Great Worship for Kids* know that's true. They've tried to consider individual differences as they've planned worship sessions. As you examine each session you'll find some activities that are easy, some that are more difficult. Some appeal to pupils who like to research or to work puzzles, and some to pupils who like to speak and act. Each session will have something that addresses the needs of each pupil.

I guess so. And even if a pupil doesn't get into the activities one week, the following week he can find something he likes. But while we're talking about the number of activities in each session, what about the number of adult leaders needed for all the small groups? There are only two of us, and we can't be everywhere!

One solution is to use a cassette recorder. Tape record instructions for one or more of the small groups and have those groups work independently. Or photocopy the instructions for pupils to read. Ask an older or more mature pupil to serve as "chairperson" of the group to keep things moving.

I've tried that. As a matter of fact, during the week before the session I contact pupils to be chairpersons. That way I can give them special instructions so they'll be prepared. And it's good to get to know the pupils better and make them feel special.

Great! And then during *Building the Theme* you can circulate between groups as they need attention. You can also choose only one or two activities to prepare in small groups, and do the rest of the session as a large group. And—though it's not ideal—you can always omit parts of *Sharing in Worship* if they can't be prepared in small groups.

I always hate to leave things out. But actually, I feel as though we get into a rut sometimes anyway, so I guess it's not so bad to drop something from time to time. We do many of the same things every week. Take music, for instance. The kids either write words for a song, sing songs, or choose songs for the group to sing. It's so predictable!

So is adult worship. Think about what is done in most churches today—the same things, often in the same order, Sunday after Sunday. Your Middlers and Juniors may not find it objectionable to do the same things over and over—they may find security in activities that are familiar to them.

I wish *I* felt more secure . . . about how to split up the pupils into small groups, I mean. The rowdy kids want to be in a group together, and then they end up wasting time and cutting up. And the shy kids just sit and look at each other for half their group time before they can get started working together. Any suggestions?

As leader you can always assign groups yourself, mixing the groups as you choose. Whenever you possibly can, however, allow the pupils to volunteer for groups they're interested in. The easiest way to do this is to have sign-up sheets. Indicate on each sheet the maximum number of pupils who may sign up so you don't have nine kids working a crossword puzzle while only two prepare to act out a Bible story. You can always choose groups at random, also—having the pupils draw numbers out of a hat or count off. The key is to vary things as much as you can, but always to do what works best with your kids in your group.

And you know, the kids I lead are . . . well, they're just great kids. I love them all.

What was that—about the kids, I mean?

I love them.

No, what you said before that.

They're great kids.

And when they worship?

What? Oh, I get it! Great kids—GREAT WORSHIP!

Try Great Worship for Kids

If you've never used *Great Worship for Kids* before, here are some things you need to know:

This book contains 13 sessions. The sessions are based on Scriptures and lessons from Standard Publishing's Middler and Junior Sunday school curriculum.

Each worship session is planned so that pupils work in small groups to prepare the elements of the worship time (call to worship, Scripture, special music, devotion, offering, Lord's Supper, prayer, or personal praise). The elements the small groups have prepared are then incorporated into the worship time.

Each weekly session is designed to last 80-95 minutes. It begins with *Transition Time*, a flexible time between Sunday school and Middler/Junior worship. This is a casual time for relaxation and conversation. It includes a rest room and drink break, as well as a game or activity that allows the children to move around. This freedom is important after the pupils have been sitting during the Sunday school hour.

Involving the children in organized activity as soon as they arrive avoids confusion and eliminates the moments you spend gathering children from the halls when you are ready to begin the worship time.

During *Launching the Theme*, the leader introduces the theme of the session to the children. This is done through a story, object lesson, or dialogue. Involving pupils during this section is a priority.

The leader also explains the small group choices and guides the pupils in choosing the groups they are interested in.

Building the Theme is the time when pupils work in their groups to prepare the elements of the worship time. Adult leaders work with the small groups to help them stay on track. Some activities are designed for specific groups of children.

E indicates the activity is easy and can be used with younger or less-mature children.

I indicates that the activity may be done independently by children who work well on their own.

A indicates that the activity is suited to the abilities of more-mature pupils.

Then during *Sharing in Worship* the large group gathers for worship time. An adult leader directs this time and integrates the small group activities so the pupils participate in worship.

Closing Moments is the flexible time between the end of Middler/Junior worship and the end of adult worship. This section lists a variety of activities, but each one can be dropped quickly and easily when the adult service is over.

Activity pages are included with each session plan. You are free to photocopy any of the pages for use with your worship group.

Unit

Session

Bible Story

Scripture

Worship Focus

Transition Time

Leader

Materials

Preparation

Procedure

Launching the Theme

Leader

Materials

Preparation

Procedure

Worship Plan Sheet

Sharing in Worship

Leader

Closing Moments

Leader

Materials

Preparation

Procedure

Building the Theme

Group 1
Materials
Preparation
Procedure
Leader

Group 2
Materials
Preparation
Procedure
Leader

Group 3
Materials
Preparation
Procedure
Leader

Group 4
Materials
Preparation
Procedure
Leader

Group 5
Materials
Preparation
Procedure
Leader

Group 6
Materials
Preparation
Procedure
Leader

Worship Plan Sheet

Bible Story: The Promised Prophet
Isaiah 40:3, 5; Luke 1:8-25

Unit 1: Trust God Who Keeps His Promises
Session 1

Worship Focus: Worship God because He keeps His promises.

A Promise Is Kept

Transition Time
10-15 minutes

Send the pupils in small groups to the rest rooms and drinking fountain. Welcome newcomers and involve everyone in the following activity.

Keeping Promises. Divide the pupils into two groups. Provide paper and a pencil or pen for each group. One pupil in each group should be the designated writer. One group of pupils will brainstorm and come up with promises that were made to them at various times in their lives. The promises could be from anyone. The other group of pupils will brainstorm times when they made promises to others, whether they kept the promises or not. After a few minutes, have both groups stop brainstorming. Have each group take a turn going down the list and checking each promise that was kept either to them or by them.

Launching the Theme
10 minutes

Which group had the most promises checked? (Allow response.) **Do you think it is easier to keep a promise you have made or have someone else keep a promise he or she made to you?** (Allow response.) **We have no control over the promises other people make to us. How does it make you feel when someone doesn't keep a promise he or she made to you?** (Allow response.) **You might feel angry or sad and it would probably be harder to believe that person if he or she ever made another promise to you.**

In today's lesson, a promise is made to a man named Zechariah that is hard for him to believe. God made the promise, however, so Zechariah should have known that it would happen. **If a promise is made by God, we never have to doubt whether or not it will be fulfilled. God always keeps His promises. Today we will worship God because He always keeps His promises.**

Briefly explain the choices of preparation for worship. Allow each child to choose the group in which he or she would like to participate.

Building the Theme
30 minutes

E easy **I** independent **A** advanced

1 Call to Worship
Pupils will write a responsive reading about God's promises. For this activity you will need copies of Activity Page 1A,

9

pencils, Bibles, and concordances.

Have the pupils look up Psalm 145:13b ("The Lord is faithful to all His promises and loving toward all He has made"). On the activity page pupils will use this verse as the response the entire group will say after each line by a member of Group 1. The pupils should use their Bibles and concordances to find promises God made either to people in the Bible or to us. A hint for doing so is at the bottom of the activity page. They may either copy the verse with a promise or put it in their own words. If the children are unfamiliar with using a concordance, some instruction from an adult will be necessary.

What does Psalm 145:13b tell us about God's promises? (He is faithful to them all.) **Do we ever need to doubt anything God promises?** (No.) **How does this make you feel?** (Allow response. Secure, safe, happy, and so on.)

During *Sharing in Worship*, the pupils will involve the entire group in a responsive reading as the Call to Worship. You may want to write out Psalm 145:13b on a chalkboard or on an overhead transparency so the large group can see the words easily.

2 Scripture

Pupils will complete a puzzle about Bible people to whom God made promises. For this activity, provide copies of Activity Page 1B, pencils, and Bibles. If the pupils in the group will be working independently, tape record or write out brief instructions for them to follow.

Have the pupils read the clues given and decide the names of the people to whom God made the promises. Pupils may use the Scripture references given if they need additional help.

What kinds of promises did God make? (Promises of the birth of sons; having many descendants; help to conquer an enemy; bringing people out of Egypt to a better land; safety; the promise He would always be with them.) **Did God fulfill all these promises?** (Yes.) **Do you think God will always fulfill His promises?** (Yes.)

During *Sharing in Worship*, the pupils will take turns reading the Scripture references and telling the names of the people to whom God made the promises.

3 Devotion

Pupils will create a puppet play showing the events of Luke 1:8-25. This activity will require Bibles and materials to create puppets, such as paper lunch sacks, markers, fabric scraps, yarn, construction paper, scissors, and glue. Use either a large cardboard box or a table turned on its side for the puppet stage.

Have the pupils look up Luke 1:8-25. They will make puppets for Zechariah, the angel Gabriel, Elizabeth, and some other people (as mentioned in verses 21, 22). During *Sharing in Worship*, the puppet play will be presented as the Devotion.

What promise was made to Zechariah? (His wife would have a son and they would name him John.) **Who made this promise to Zechariah?** (The angel Gabriel was the messenger from God to Zechariah.) **Did Zechariah have trouble believing? Why?** (Yes. He doubted and asked the angel how it could be possible. It was probably hard to believe because he thought he and Elizabeth were too old to have children.) **Was the promise fulfilled?** (Yes!)

4 Scripture

Pupils will personalize Scriptural promises and illustrate favorite ones. For this activity pupils will need copies of Activity Page 1C, Bibles, pencils, and crayons or markers.

Begin by having the pupils look up the verses given. Then have the pupil rewrite each verse using his or her name in it. At the bottom of the page each pupil may illustrate his or her favorite promise.

During *Sharing in Worship*, the pupils will take turns reading the promises and sharing their illustrations.

What are some of the promises God has made to you? (I am forgiven and purified. I have been made holy. God will never leave me. I have eternal life. Jesus is coming soon. If I suffer for what is right, I am blessed.) **Are these important promises to you? Why?** (Allow response.) **Does God always keep His promises?** (Yes.)

5 Music A
Pupils will write a song about God's promises. This activity will require Bibles, pencils, and paper.

Have the pupils begin by reading Psalms 119:103, 140, 148; and 145:13. Have them discuss what these verses mean. Then have them choose a tune to a familiar chorus. They will write words about God's promises to sing to the familiar tune. They will sing the song as special music during *Sharing in Worship*.

What do these verse tell you about God's promises? (They are sweet. The promises have been tested and are loved. I should meditate on God's promises. God is faithful to all His promises.) **Are God's promises special?** (Yes, He always keeps them.) **What does it mean to meditate on God's promises?** (To think about them.)

6 Personal Praise E
Pupils will make posters that show how they feel about the fact that God always keeps His promises. Provide Bibles, freezer paper or shelf paper, tempera paints, sponges cut into various shapes, paper bowls, old shirts for smocks, and water.

First, ask the pupils to look up Joshua 23:14. Then have them use the sponges and paint to create posters that show how they feel because they know God always keeps His promises. During *Sharing in Worship*, have the verse read aloud by a good reader. Then have each pupil in the group show his poster and explain how this verse makes him feel.

What does this verse tell you about all of the promises God made to Joshua and the Israelites? (Not one of the promises failed. Every promise had been fulfilled.) **Does God always keep His promises?** (Yes.) **Does this mean He will keep every promise we read in the Bible?** (Yes.) **How does this make you feel?** (Allow response.)

Sharing in Worship
20-25 minutes

If you did not have pupils do all the activities, plan to present them yourself or have another adult or two help you. Omit any activity that is too involved for you to do without help from the group.

Call to Worship
Group 1 has prepared a responsive reading for us. Have one of the pupils from the group explain to the others what words they will speak and when they are to speak. Then continue with the reading.

Scripture
Group 2 did some research to find people in the Bible who received promises from God. Have the pupils take turns reading each Scripture passage aloud.

Devotion
Group 3 has prepared a puppet play for us about someone who received a special promise from God. Have the pupils present their puppet play.

It was probably hard for Zechariah to take in all that happened while he was in the temple. Why did he doubt the promise the angel Gabriel told him? (He thought he and his wife were too old to be having a baby.) **Did the promise happen?** (Yes.) **Who made the promise to**

Zechariah? (God, through His messenger Gabriel.)

We never need to doubt any of God's promises. In Psalm 145:13, we read that God is faithful to all His promises. Every promise from God will be fulfilled. We can read about how some of God's promises have already been fulfilled, such as the one to Zechariah. This should give us confidence and hope that all the other promises we find from God will also be fulfilled. For example, when He promises forgiveness and eternal life with Him through Jesus, we can know these promises will be kept. We can trust God and be secure in knowing He will keep His word. Praise God that He keeps His promises!

Lord's Supper
God promises us forgiveness of our sins through the blood shed by His Son, Jesus. As we take the Lord's Supper today, let's remember this special promise.

Offering
God promises to provide our needs. When we give our offerings to Him, it helps provide for some of the needs of others.

Scripture
Group 4 found some promises God made to them. Have the pupils take turns reading their paraphrased verses and displaying their illustrations.

Music
Group 5 wrote a song about God's promises. They will sing it for us now.

Personal Praise
Posters were made by the pupils in Group 6 to show how they feel about knowing that God keeps all His promises. Have each child take a turn to explain his or her poster.

Close with a prayer of praise that God always keeps His promises.

Closing Moments
10-15 minutes

Christmas Cards. Have art supplies, such as construction paper, glue, scissors, markers, glitter, and so on. Let each pupil make a Christmas card that tells about a promise God made or how God keeps His promises. Encourage the pupils to tell to whom they will give their cards.

ALL: _____
_____ (Psalm 145:13b).

SPEAKER 1: _____
_____

ALL: _____
_____ (Psalm 145:13b).

SPEAKER 2: _____
_____

ALL: _____
_____ (Psalm 145:13b).

SPEAKER 1: _____
_____

ALL: _____
_____ (Psalm 145:13b).

You Can Depend on It!

Write a responsive reading using your Bible. You'll also need a concordance. Use Scriptures that tell about promises God made to people in the Bible, or promises He has made to you. Use Psalm 145:13b as a response to each promise. Assign parts and practice the reading in your group.

Hint: Look up the words *promise*, *promised*, and *promises* in your concordance. Or think of Bible stories you know in which God made a promise to people like Noah, Abraham, Hannah, or David.

© 1994 by The STANDARD PUBLISHING COMPANY. Permission is granted to photocopy this page for ministry purposes only—not for resale.

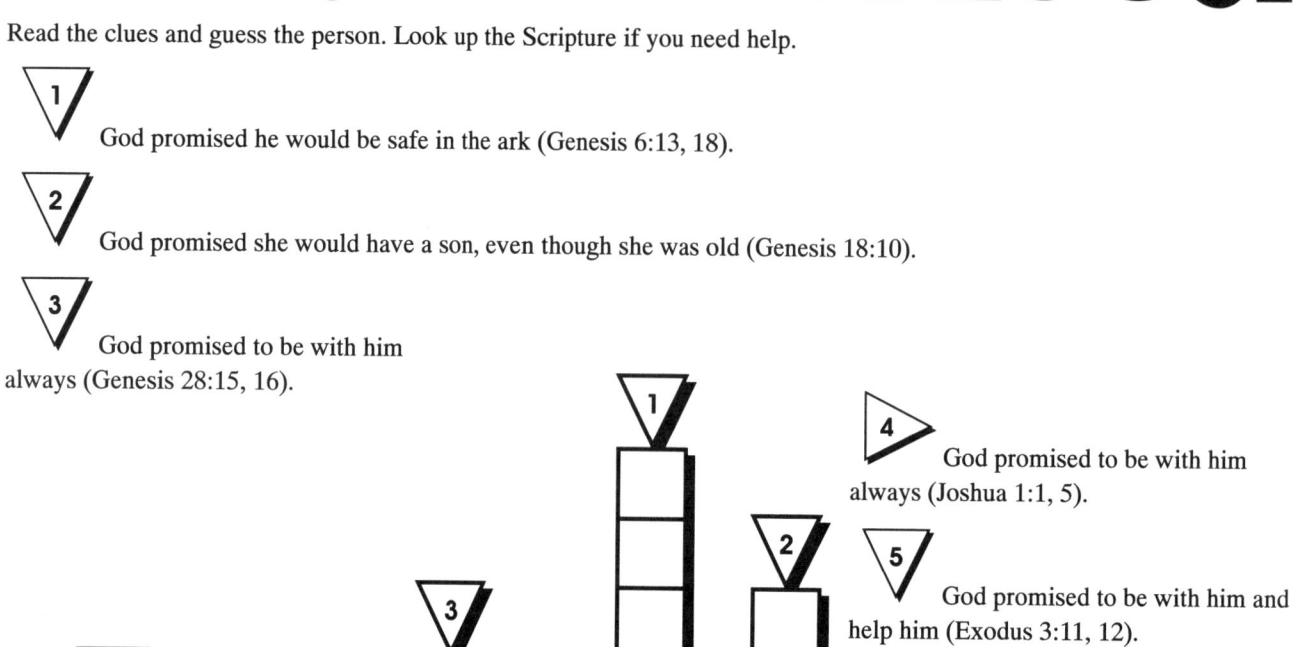

God Promised

Read the clues and guess the person. Look up the Scripture if you need help.

▽1 God promised he would be safe in the ark (Genesis 6:13, 18).

▽2 God promised she would have a son, even though she was old (Genesis 18:10).

▽3 God promised to be with him always (Genesis 28:15, 16).

▷4 God promised to be with him always (Joshua 1:1, 5).

▷5 God promised to be with him and help him (Exodus 3:11, 12).

▷6 God promised she would have a son, Jesus (Luke 1:30, 31).

▷7 God promised his wife would have a son (Luke 1:11-13).

▷8 God promised she would have a son (Luke 1:11-13).

▽9 God promised he would conquer Sisera (Judges 4:6, 7).

▷10 God promised he would have many descendants (Genesis 22:15-18).

▷11 God promised he would lead these people out of Egypt (Exodus 3:16, 17).

1B © 1994 by The STANDARD PUBLISHING COMPANY. Permission is granted to photocopy this page for ministry purposes only—not for resale.

Promises to Me!

Look up the Scriptures. Rewrite each verse using your name. Then choose one of your favorite promises and illustrate it in the space given. One paraphrase has been done for you.

Hebrews 10:10

1 John 5:13

Revelation 22:12 *I am coming soon! I bring my reward, and I will give to Jenna according to what she has done.*

1 Peter 3:14

Hebrews 13:5b

1 John 1:9

© 1994 by The STANDARD PUBLISHING COMPANY. Permission is granted to photocopy this page for ministry purposes only—not for resale. 1C

Bible Story: The Promised Son
Isaiah 9:6, 7; Luke 1:26-38

Unit 1: Trust God Who Keeps His Promises
Session 2

Worship Focus: Worship God because He knows the future.

The Savior Is Coming

Transition Time
10-15 minutes

Send the pupils in small groups to the rest rooms and drinking fountain. Welcome newcomers and involve everyone in the following activity.

When Did It Happen? Before class begins, write a different historical event on each of several index cards. (For example: Abraham Lincoln is president; man walked on the moon; Jesus was born; Noah built the ark; Operation Desert Storm; Columbus discovered America; penicillin was discovered; the Great Depression; and so on.) Make sure you have a card for each pupil. Tell the children to stand in the correct chronological order of the events listed on their cards. When the pupils think they are in correct order, check their accuracy.

Launching the Theme
10 minutes

Ask the pupils to suggest some events that might happen in the future. Let pupils name some events, then point out that no one knows the future but God.

Why could you put the historical events in order? (Allow response. They have already occurred.) **What are some events that are going to occur in the future?** (Allow response. Pupils may list events such as graduation from school, going to college, getting married, having children, and so on.) **Many of these events will probably happen, but do any of you know for certain they will?** (Allow response.)

In today's lesson, God tells Mary, through the angel Gabriel, that she is going to have a baby. No human being could tell Mary what was going to happen in her future. Only God could. God also knows every detail of your future. Today we will worship God because He knows the future.

Briefly explain the choices of preparation for worship. Allow pupils to choose the groups in which they would like to participate.

Building the Theme
30 minutes

E easy **I** independent **A** advanced

1 Call to Worship **E**
Pupils will create a banner praising God for knowing their future. You will need a large piece of felt or similar fabric, scraps of felt and/or fabric, scissors, glue, glitter, yarn, and Bibles.

16

To begin, have the pupils read John 14:2, 3, and 6. The pupils will discuss what the verses mean. Then they will create a banner praising God for knowing their future. During *Sharing in Worship*, the pupils will display the banner as a good reader reads John 14:2, 3, and 6 aloud This will serve as the Call to Worship.

What do these verses tell us about our future? (Jesus is going to prepare a place for us in His Father's house [Heaven]. Jesus will come back to get us to take us to be with Him there.) **What is the only way we can get to this place and be with our Father?** (Through Jesus.) **Did God know we would need a Savior in order for us to be with Him?** (Yes.) **Are you glad God knows your future? Why?** (Allow response. God knew I would need a Savior and provided His Son Jesus to fill that need. God has told me where I will spend eternity so I don't need to worry about that.) **Let's make a banner praising our wonderful God for knowing what we need and providing His Son for us.**

2 Devotion

Pupils will prepare a taped conversation between Mary and the angel Gabriel. This activity will require Bibles, paper, pencils, a tape recorder, and a blank tape.

Have the pupils turn to Luke 1:26-38 in their Bibles and read the account of the angel Gabriel telling Mary she would bear the Son of God. If younger children are working on the activity, you may want to shorten the Scriptural account to verses 26-33 and 38. After the pupils have read the passage, have them write the conversation between Gabriel and Mary in their own words. Then tape record the event. You will need voices for the angel Gabriel, Mary, and a narrator. For the Devotion during *Sharing in Worship*, pupils will play the tape as the others listen.

What did God tell Mary about her future? (She was highly favored and God was with her. She would have a son and name Him Jesus. He would be the Son of God.) **Who was the only One who could have known Mary's future?** (God. He sent His message through the angel Gabriel.) **Did Mary have a baby son and name Him Jesus?** (Yes.) **Does God always know the future?** (Yes.)

3 Scripture

Pupils will research Scripture and also write personal testimonies. Pupils will need copies of Activity Page 2A, pencils, and Bibles. If pupils will be working independently, either tape record or write out brief instructions for them. Make sure you include the questions given below to help pupils understand the activity. If you are taping, you may want to pause after a question, then give the answer before going to the next question.

Have the pupils turn to Isaiah 9:6 and read the verse. Then have them complete the activity. During *Sharing in Worship*, the pupils will take turns reading their work.

What are the four names for Jesus found in Isaiah 9:6? (Wonderful Counselor, Mighty God, Everlasting Father, Prince of Peace.) **These names describe the nature of Jesus. Think about Jesus' earthly ministry. Can you tell me a time when Jesus was a Wonderful Counselor?** (When He spoke with Nicodemus or with the rich young ruler.) **When did Jesus act as Mighty God?** (When He made Lazarus come alive; when He calmed the storm.) **When was He the Everlasting Father?** (When He arose from the dead to be alive forever.) **When was the Prince of Peace side of Jesus evident?** (In John 14:27 He talks about His peace.) **Has there ever been a time in your life when Jesus particularly fit one of these names?** (Allow response.)

4 Scripture

Pupils will research Scripture to discover

evidence that God knows the future. For this activity, you will need to provide copies of Activity Page 2B, pencils, and Bibles.

To begin, have the pupils look up the verses given to find what God knew or knows about the future. During *Sharing in Worship*, the pupils can take turns reading what they wrote for each Scripture passage.

What were some of the things God knew about the future in the Old Testament? (He told Deborah that Sisera would be conquered. He told Moses He would release Israel from their bondage in Egypt. Through a dream, God told Pharaoh about the famine that was to come to Egypt. He told Noah about the destruction of the earth by a flood. He told Abram he would become a great nation and all people would be blessed through him.) **What were some of the things God knew about the future in the New Testament?** (Jesus knew He would be killed and would arise after three days. Jesus knew Peter would deny Him. Jesus knew Judas would betray Him. God knows when heaven and earth will pass away.) **If God knew all these things would happen—and they did—does God know the future of people today?** (Yes.)

5 Personal Praise A

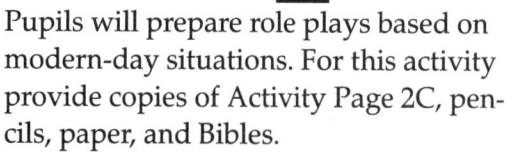

Pupils will prepare role plays based on modern-day situations. For this activity provide copies of Activity Page 2C, pencils, paper, and Bibles.

Divide pupils into three groups and assign each group one of the situations from the activity page. Each group should read its situation, discuss possible endings, then write the best ending. The role play should show that people don't need to be afraid of the future because God knows their future. The Scripture references given should help with this. Each role play should end with a praise statement. The role plays will be presented after the Offering during *Sharing in Worship*.

If pupils need help, ask these questions before they begin to write. **In the first situation, what is Andrea afraid of?** (Not having money for things the family needs.) **What does God know about Andrea's future?** (He knows her every need. He knows the needs of the birds and flowers and provides for them, so surely He will care for Andrea.) **What is Joshua afraid of?** (He is afraid of dying.) **What does God know about Joshua's future?** (God is preparing a place for Joshua in Heaven. Heaven is a wonderful place!) **What is Cassandra fearing about the future?** (She is afraid of kids making fun of her for being a Christian.) **What does God know about her future?** (He knows that persecution will come and if she stands firm she will be saved.)

6 Personal Praise

Pupils will paint pictures to praise God for knowing their future. Provide watercolors, brushes, water, newsprint, old shirts to use as smocks, and Bibles for this activity.

First, have the pupils read Luke 1:26-38. Lead a short discussion about how Mary must have felt when God told her what was in her future. Then discuss how they feel about God knowing their future. After the discussion, the pupils will paint watercolor pictures expressing their praise to God for knowing their future. During *Sharing in Worship*, the pupils will take turns showing their paintings and explaining them.

How do you think Mary felt when the angel appeared to her? (Frightened.) **After the angel gave Mary the message about her future, how do you think she felt?** (Allow response.) **God sent His Son because He also knows our future. He knew we would need a Savior. How do you feel knowing God knows all your needs and provides them for you?** (Allow response.)

Sharing in Worship

20-25 minutes

If you did not have pupils do all the activities, plan to present them yourself or have another adult or two help you. Omit any activity that is too involved for you to do without help from the group.

Call to Worship
Group 1 created a banner to share with us. Have a pupil read John 14:2, 3, and 6 aloud as the group displays the banner.

Devotion
Group 2 has prepared a tape of the conversation between the angel Gabriel and Mary. Play the tape and then continue with the devotion.

God knew what was going to happen in Mary's life. He knew she would bear His Son, Jesus. God sent His Son to earth because He also knew our future. God knew none of us could live a perfect life and never sin. He knew none of us would be able to enter into Heaven without a Savior. God loves us so very much that He sent His Son to die for us so we would be able to go to our special home in Heaven with Him. Jesus has prepared a special place for us. He knows every detail of our future. We don't have to worry because God knows our future and has provided what we need.

Scripture
The pupils in Group 3 wrote about Biblical names that describe Jesus. Have a pupil read Isaiah 9:6 aloud. Then have children take turns reading what they wrote.

Scripture
Group 4 did some research to find verses that show God knows the future. Have pupils take turns reading aloud their findings.

Lord's Supper
The Bible tells us that God knew we would need a Savior. He sent His Son, Jesus, to be the sacrifice for our sins. As we take the Lord's Supper, let's be thankful that God knew we would need a Savior and sent His very own Son for that purpose.

Offering
Giving our offerings is one way we have to thank God for knowing our future and providing for our needs.

Personal Praise
Group 5 has prepared three short skits to show that we don't need to fear because God knows our future. Have pupils present their skits.

Personal Praise
Have pupils in Group 6 share their watercolor paintings and describe how they feel about God knowing their future.

Closing Moments

10-15 minutes

Picture That! Provide crayons or markers and paper so the pupils can draw pictures of themselves twenty years from now. Discuss how it is fun to think about what we might be doing twenty years from now, but that only God knows our future for certain.

1
Name of Jesus:
_____
_____
John 3:1-21
Mark 10:17-22

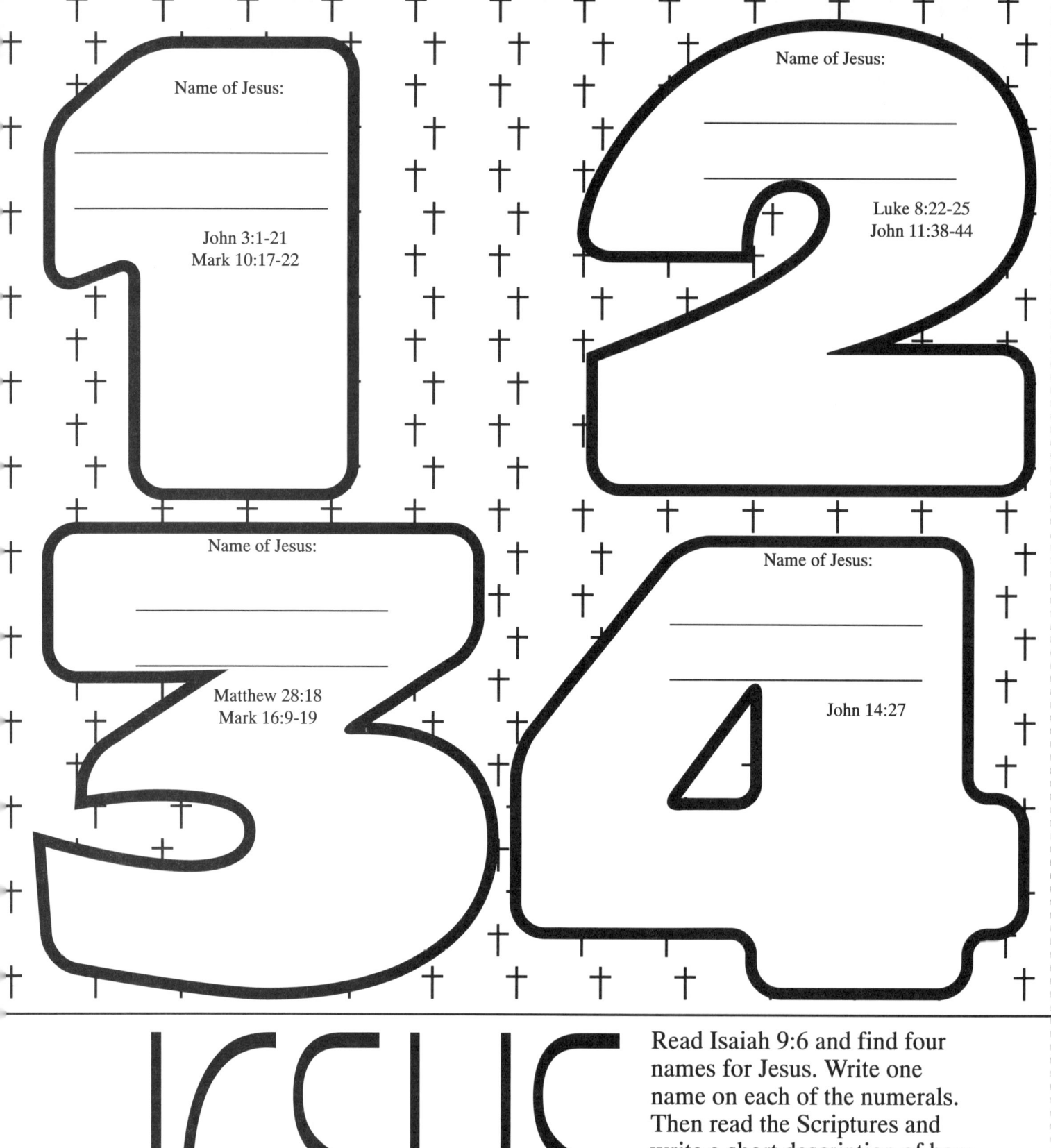

2
Name of Jesus:
_____
_____
Luke 8:22-25
John 11:38-44

3
Name of Jesus:
_____
_____
Matthew 28:18
Mark 16:9-19

4
Name of Jesus:
_____
_____
John 14:27

JESUS

Read Isaiah 9:6 and find four names for Jesus. Write one name on each of the numerals. Then read the Scriptures and write a short description of how Jesus showed himself to fit the name. If you wish, you can describe a time in your life when you discovered how that name is appropriate for Jesus.

2A © 1994 by The STANDARD PUBLISHING COMPANY. Permission is granted to photocopy this page for ministry purposes only—not for resale.

What's Ahead?

God Knows the Future

Look up the verses to find out what God knew or knows about the future. The first one has been done for you.

1. Joshua 6:2-5—*God told Joshua how Jericho would be defeated.*

2. Mark 8:31

3. Judges 4:4-7

4. Exodus 6:6-8

5. Mark 14:30

6. Mark 14:18, 42-45

7. Genesis 41:25-27

8. Mark 13:31, 32

9. Genesis 6:13, 17

10. Genesis 12:2, 3

© 1994 by The STANDARD PUBLISHING COMPANY. Permission is granted to photocopy this page for ministry purposes only—not for resale.

Don't Fear the Future

Write endings to the situations to show how the person involved doesn't need to fear the future. Look up the Scripture references before you write.

1. Andrea's grandma has come to live at Andrea's house because she is too sick to live alone anymore. Grandma requires a lot of care and has a lot of medical bills. Andrea heard her dad say he's worried the family won't have enough money to buy food or clothes. Now Andrea's worried too. (Matthew 6:31, 32)

2. Joshua watches TV a lot. He likes real-life action shows, like *Rescue 911* or *Search and Rescue*. He's seen stories about kids who had swimming pool accidents or were hit by cars, who were seriously hurt or ill. Lately Joshua's feeling afraid he will get sick or be in a car accident. He's afraid he will die. (John 14:1, 2; Revelation 21:3, 4, 18-21)

3. Every day when Cassandra gets on the bus, some of the older kids say mean things to her because she's a Christian. They laugh at her because they know she follows Jesus. Now Cassandra's afraid to get on the bus. She wants her mom to drive her to school. (Mark 13:13)

Bible Story: God Sends a Prophet
Luke 1:57-65, 67, 76-78, 80

Unit 1: Trust God Who Keeps His Promises
Session 3

Worship Focus: Worship God because we can trust Him.

A Message to Israel

Transition Time
10-15 minutes

Send the pupils in small groups to the rest rooms and drinking fountain. Welcome newcomers and involve everyone in the following activity.

Promise Search. Before class list commands on a chalkboard or poster board, leaving enough space across from each command to write a promise. (For example: Buy this soap. Buy this detergent. Buy these shoes. Eat these foods. Join this health club. Chew this gum. Use this shampoo. Buy this car. Wear these clothes. Take this pain reliever.) Have the pupils think about times they have seen or heard commercials on TV or radio for similar products or advertisements in magazines or newspapers. Have the pupils write what they are promised if they buy a certain product. For example: Buy these shoes—Jump higher or run faster than anyone else.

Launching the Theme
10 minutes

Do you hear a lot of promises during a day? Where do you hear people promise you something? (Allow response.) **People who are trying to sell something make many promises, as we learned during our "Promise Search." But, can we trust these promises completely? Do they always happen?** (No.) **What about promises made to you by your friends or brothers or sisters?** (Allow response.) **What about promises your parents make to you?** (Allow response.) **People don't always keep their promises. Sometimes they promise things just to get you to do or buy something. Other times they may not be able to keep a promise. So, we can't always trust a product, or even a person sometimes.**

In our lesson two weeks ago, we praised God for always keeping His promises. Last week we talked about the fact that God knows what is in the future. Today, we will see how God kept His promise to Zechariah to give him a son. When the angel told Zechariah he would have a son, he also told him his son would prepare the people for the Lord. God kept that promise when Zechariah's son, John, was born. We know John did prepare the people for Jesus. The Bible tells us that God kept His promise to Zechariah and we know we can trust God always to keep His promises. We know God cannot lie. We can be assured every promise God has made will be kept. Today we will worship God because we can trust Him.

Briefly explain the choices of preparation for worship. Allow the children to choose the groups in which they would like to participate.

Building the Theme
30 minutes

E easy   **I** independent   **A** advanced

1 Call to Worship
Pupils will choose several "promise" songs and sing them for the large group. Pupils will need paper, pencils, hymnals or chorus books, and Bibles.

Have the pupils look up Joshua 23:14. ("You know with all your heart and soul that not one of all the good promises the Lord your God gave you has failed. Every promise has been fulfilled; not one has failed.") After a discussion about this verse, have the pupils look through the hymnals and/or chorus books to find songs about God's promises. After making a list, the pupils will choose one or two songs to practice to sing as special music during *Sharing in Worship*. (Suggestions: "Standing on the Promises," "Jesus, Lord of Promises," "A Promise Is a Promise.")

Who is speaking in Joshua 23:14? (Joshua.) **To whom is Joshua speaking?** (The leaders of Israel.) **What is he telling these people about God's promises?** (God had kept every promise ever made to them.) **Did God ever fail to keep any promise?** (No.) **The Bible tells us God never changes. He has kept every promise He has made and we can trust Him to keep His promises.**

2 Devotion
Pupils will design a mural to depict the story of John's birth. You will need to provide copies of Activity Page 3A, Bibles, pencils, newsprint, and markers or crayons.

The pupils should look up Luke 1:57-80, read the verses, then order the events found on the activity page. After pupils have the events in mind, they are to create a mural depicting these events. During *Sharing in Worship*, the pupils will take turns reading the events aloud in the correct order while displaying the mural.

Focus a discussion on helping the pupils understand the events that occurred. **What had God promised Zechariah and Elizabeth?** (They would have a son who would prepare the way of the Lord.) **When Zechariah was told this would happen and he didn't believe, what happened to him?** (He couldn't speak.) **Did God's promise come true?** (Yes. Elizabeth had a son.) **The people assumed the baby would be named Zechariah after his father. Why was he named John?** (The angel told him he was to name the child John.) **When Zechariah told everyone the baby would be named John, what happened?** (Zechariah began to speak and praise God. Then Zechariah prophesied that John would prepare the way of the Lord.) **Did God keep His promise?** (Yes.) **Do you think Zechariah learned that he could always trust God? Can we trust Him?** (Yes!)

3 Scripture
Pupils will read "promise" Scripture verses and illustrate them. Provide Bibles, construction paper, markers or crayons, and a stapler.

Ask the pupils to look up the following verses and write the promise given in each verse on a separate piece of construction paper. Each child will receive one verse. Verses are: 2 Chronicles 7:14; Philippians 4:19; Isaiah 49:15; John 3:16; Titus 1:2. Each pupil will illustrate the promise on his or her paper. After the pupils have written the promises and illustrated them, staple the pages together to form a "Promise Book." During *Sharing in Worship,* each pupil will read his or her verse, name the promise, and share the illustration created to go with the promise.

What does God promise in 2 Chronicles 7:14? (If people will humble themselves and pray and turn from their wicked ways, God will forgive their sin and heal their land.) **What is promised in Philippians 4:19?** (God will meet all our needs.) **In Isaiah 49:15?** (God will not forget you.) **In John 3:16?** (He who believes will have everlasting life.) **In Titus 1:2?** (Eternal life.)

4 Personal Praise A

Pupils will list promises from God and write personal praise statements. Pupils will need Bibles, concordances, paper, and pencils.

Have the pupils name promises God has made to us. Make a list of these promises on the chalkboard or a poster board. Pupils may use Bibles or concordances if they need help. After making a list, have each pupil choose a promise, and write one or two paragraphs telling why it is important to him or her to be able to trust God to keep this promise. During *Sharing in Worship*, pupils will take turns reading their promises and their reasons.

What has God promised you? (God provides needs; forgives sins; eternal life; Jesus is coming again; the Holy Spirit; His care, and so on.) **Can you trust God to keep these promises? Why are these important promises to you?** (I don't need to worry or fear the future. I can be secure in God's love and care. I can trust Him to take care of things that are out of my control.)

5 Personal Praise E

Pupils will create a mobile to show that we can always trust God. Pupils will need magazines, construction paper, scissors, a hanger, yarn cut in various lengths, glue, and Bibles.

Have the pupils look through the magazines to find advertisements that make promises about various products. Pupils are to cut out the ads and glue each one to a shape cut out of construction paper. On the other side of the paper the pupil will write a promise from God's Word. (You may want to provide the Scripture verses used in activity 3.) Help pupils attach yarn to the paper shapes.

What kinds of things do advertisers promise? (Allow response. Look better; be smarter; be more popular; have more friends, and so on.) **Can you trust all these products to do what the ads promise?** (No.) **What are some promises God tells us?** (Allow response.) **Does God always keep His promises?** (Yes.) **What does this tell you?** (I can always trust God!)

During *Sharing in Worship*, each child will take a turn showing his or her ad and saying, "(Advertiser's name) claims that _____." Then turn the paper over to God's promise and say, "But I know I can trust God to _____." After saying this the pupil will attach his shape to the hanger. After pupils have all had turns, they will have created a mobile to display in the classroom.

6 Prayer I

Each pupil will write a short prayer praising God that He can always be trusted. Provide copies of Activity Page 3B, pencils, and Bibles.

Pupils will look up the Scriptures given and write the promises they find. Then in the space provided, have them write specific times when God kept those promises to them. Following that, a sentence prayer should be written praising God because He can always be trusted to do what He says He will do. An example for the Scripture containing the promise of forgiveness could be a time when a pupil disobeyed his parents. His sentence prayer could be, "Thank You, God, for keeping Your promise to forgive me when I disobeyed my mom. I praise You, God, that I can always trust You." During *Sharing in*

Worship, the pupils will take turns reading aloud what they have written.

Sharing in Worship
20-25 minutes

Call to Worship
Group 1 prepared some songs for us about God's promises. Have a pupil read Joshua 23:14 aloud and then have the group sing the song(s) they practiced as special music. **Because God always keeps His promises, we know we can always trust Him.**

Devotion
Group 2 prepared a mural depicting events from the story of the birth of John. Have pupils read the events aloud in proper order while displaying the mural.

God promised Zechariah he would have a son. God said that Zechariah's son would prepare the people for the coming of the Lord. When Zechariah did not trust God's message, he was told he would be silent until after the baby was born. **Did God keep His promises to Zechariah?** (Yes.) **Do you think Zechariah always trusted God after that?**

God has always kept His promises. In Joshua 23:14 we read that God kept every promise He ever made. We know God does not change and God cannot lie. God continues to keep His promises to us. He promises to provide our needs. He promises us forgiveness of our sins through Jesus. He promises us eternal life with Him in Heaven through Jesus. He promises us many things. Because He has always kept His promises, we can trust Him.

Scripture
Group 3 illustrated some of God's promises to us. Have the pupils read their verses and share their illustrations.

Lord's Supper
We have heard about some of the promises God has made to us. A very special one is the promise of forgiveness and eternal life. This is possible because of Jesus' death on the cross and His resurrection. As we take the Lord's Supper, let's thank God for His promises, and ask Him to help us always trust Him.

Offering
God has given us more than we could ever repay. But we can give our offerings to God to thank Him for all of His promises and to show that we trust Him.

Personal Praise
Group 4 wrote some things about why God's promises are important to them. Have each pupil read his paragraphs aloud.

Personal Praise
Have pupils from Group 5 share their advertisement/God's promises project as explained earlier. After each child shows his, have him attach it to the hanger to create the classroom mobile.

Prayer
Group 6 has written prayers to thank God for keeping specific promises, and praising Him for being trustworthy. Have pupils take turns reading their prayers aloud. Close with a brief prayer praising God because He can always be trusted.

Closing Moments
10-15 minutes

Ads You Can Trust. Have the pupils write or draw advertisements telling what God's promises can do for people. Provide paper, markers, and pens or pencils.

Number 9

Read Luke 1:57-80 in your Bible. Fill in the blanks, then number the nine events in the correct order.

☐ People made signs to _____ to see what he wanted to name the baby.

☐ The neighbors of Zechariah and Elizabeth were all _____ and talked about these strange events.

☐ _____ grew and became strong in spirit.

☐ The baby was brought to be circumcised on the _____ day.

☐ _____ was immediately able to _____ and began praising God.

☐ _____ asked for a writing tablet and wrote, "_____ _____ _____ _____."

☐ _____ had a son.

☐ Zechariah was filled with the _____ _____ and prophesied that _____ would prepare the way for the Lord.

☐ Elizabeth said to name the baby _____ instead of naming him _____ after his father.

© 1994 by The STANDARD PUBLISHING COMPANY. Permission is granted to photocopy this page for ministry purposes only—not for resale. **3A**

A PROMISE IS A PROMISE

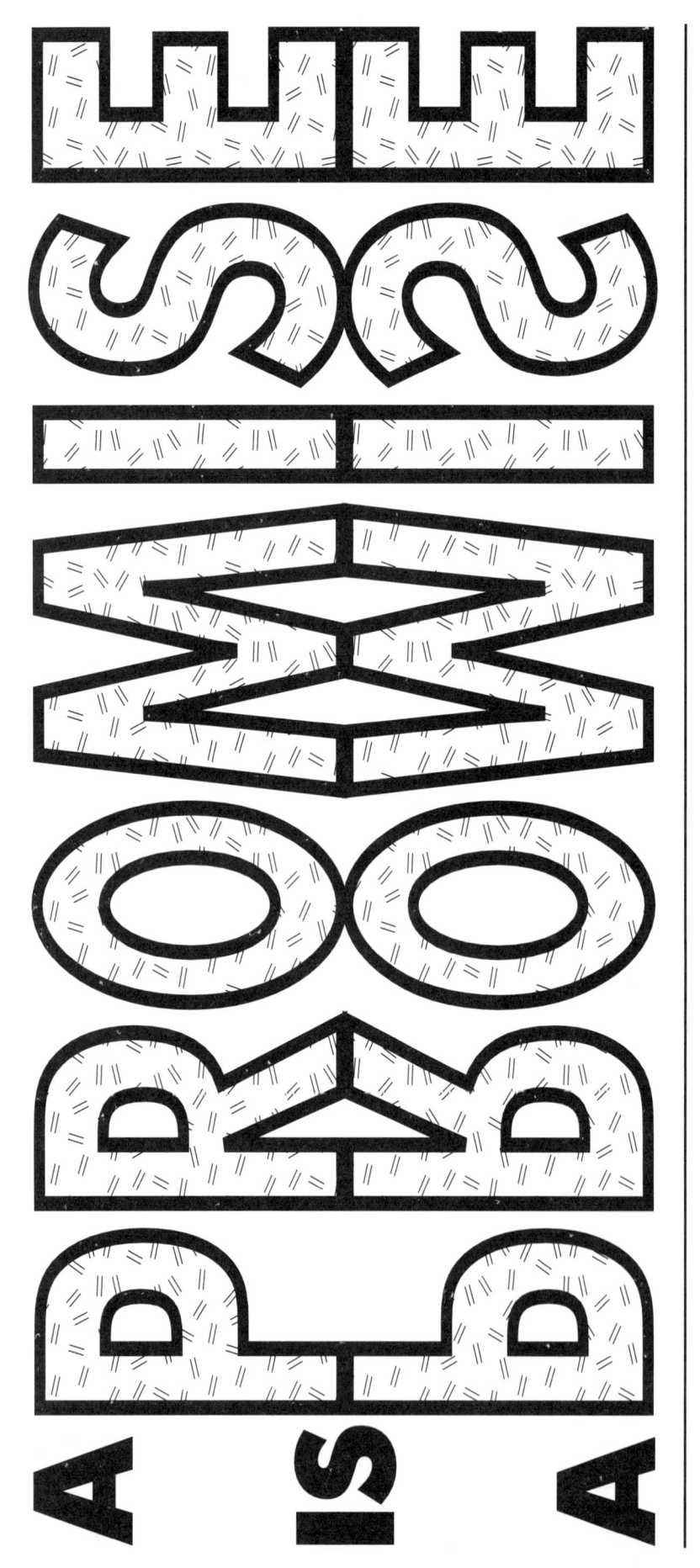

Look up these Scriptures. Identify the promise of God, and think of a way God has kept that promise to you. Write a sentence thanking God for keeping His promise at a specific time in your life.

1 John 1:9

Philippians 4:19

Deuteronomy 31:6

Bible Story: God Sends a Savior
Luke 2:1-20

Unit 1: Trust God Who Keeps His Promises
Session 4

Worship Focus: Worship God because He gave us the gift of His Son.

The Savior Is Here

Transition Time
10-15 minutes

Send pupils in small groups to the rest rooms and drinking fountain. Welcome newcomers and involve everyone in the following activity.

Christmas A-B-C. Divide the pupils into two teams. Provide a sheet of poster board and a marker for each team. Tell pupils on one team to list gifts they have given or received for Christmas, one for each letter of the alphabet. (Example: a—airplane, b—bicycle, c—candy, and so on.) Have the other team list words associated with the birth of Jesus for each letter of the alphabet. (Example: a—angel, b—baby, c—Christ, and so on.) Allow pupils approximately ten minutes to complete their lists. Then tape the two poster boards to a wall, side by side, so everyone may see both posters.

Launching the Theme
10 minutes

When someone says the word *Christmas*, which list comes into your mind? When we think of Christmas it is easy to begin thinking about gifts. We think about what we are going to give to people and we like to think about special gifts we hope to receive. All of you know the real reason we celebrate Christmas. Who can tell me? (Allow response.) **Yes, we are celebrating the birth of Jesus. Christmas is about a gift, a very special Gift. Jesus was not just another baby born into this world. He is God's Son. God sent Jesus to this world, to you and me, as a very special gift, for a special purpose—to bring us eternal life. No gift we have ever received or will ever receive in the future can compare to the gift of God's Son. Today we will worship God because He gave us the gift of His Son.**

Briefly explain the choices of preparation for worship. Allow the pupils to choose the groups in which they would like to participate.

Building the Theme
30 minutes

E easy **I** independent **A** advanced

1 Call to Worship
Pupils will put together a collage to show ways we can praise God for the gift of His Son, Jesus. Pupils will need Bibles, poster board, scissors, glue, old magazines and take-home papers, and markers.

Have the pupils look up Luke 2:13, 14, and 20. They will observe how the angels and the shepherds praised God for the birth of Jesus.

Focus a discussion on ways we can praise or glorify God. **How did the angels praise God?** (They used words.) **Why did the shepherds praise God?** (For all the things they had heard or seen.) **What does it mean to praise God?** (To tell God how special He is.) **Do you have any reasons to praise God? What are they?** (Allow response.) **What are some ways you can tell God He is special?** (We can tell Him with words; sing to Him; write prayers or poems to Him or about Him; draw pictures for Him; make something for Him, and so on.) **Does God want us to praise Him?** (Yes.)

After your discussion, have the pupils create a collage showing the various ways we can praise God for the gift of His Son. They may either use the markers and draw ways or cut out pictures from magazines and old take-home papers and glue them on the poster board. During *Sharing in Worship,* the pupils will read aloud Luke 2:13, 14, and 20 and then take turns telling ways they can praise God as they display their collage.

2 Devotion

Pupils will tell the story of the birth of Jesus using the dioramas they will put together beforehand. You will need to provide Bibles, a shoebox for each child, markers, construction paper, glue, scissors, and clay.

Before the pupils begin this project, have them read the account of Jesus' birth in Luke 2:1-20. With the pupils' help, divide the story into scenes. Then have each pupil create a diorama showing one scene from the account. During *Sharing in Worship,* the pupils will retell the story using their dioramas as visual aids.

Why were Mary and Joseph traveling to Bethlehem? (Everyone had to return to his hometown to register for a census. Joseph was from Bethlehem.) **What special event happened while they were there?** (Mary gave birth to Jesus.) **Why was baby Jesus placed in a manger?** (There was no room in the inn.) **What did nearby shepherds see?** (Angels came and told them of Jesus' birth. The angels praised God.) **What did the shepherds do after the angels left?** (Went to see Jesus and praised God.)

3 Music E

Pupils will prepare to lead the large group in singing several well-known Christmas carols. For this activity you will need copies of Activity Page 4A, pencils, and Bibles

Have the pupils look up and read the verses given on the activity page. Then have them match the verses with the appropriate Christmas carols. After they have completed this activity, pupils should practice singing the first stanzas of each carol. During *Sharing in Worship,* this group will lead the others in a time of praise singing.

What do the verses in Micah tell us about Jesus? (The ruler of Israel, the Lord, will come from the town of Bethlehem.) **Which song fits here?** ("O Little Town of Bethlehem.") **What does Luke 2:6, 7 tell us about Jesus?** (He was wrapped in cloths and laid in a manger since there was no room for them in the inn.) **What song tells us this?** ("Away in a Manger.") **What does Luke 2:10-14 tell us about Jesus?** (The angels praised God.) **Which song describes this scene?** ("Hark! the Herald Angels Sing.") **What does Philippians 2:9-11 tell us about Jesus?** (Jesus would be exalted as Christ the Lord.) **Now what song?** ("Joy to the World!")

4 Scripture

Pupils will research Scriptures to help them express reasons why Jesus is a special gift. For this activity, pupils will need

copies of Activity Page 4B, pencils, and Bibles.

First, have the pupils look up the verses given on the activity page. After each verse, pupils are to write something they read about why Jesus is a special gift. During *Sharing in Worship*, the pupils will take turns reading the verses and saying what they wrote about Jesus.

What kinds of things did you find about Jesus that make Him a special gift? (He died for us; He forgives sins; no condemnation; we have peace with God because of Him; He is "God with us"; Jesus' blood purifies us; He brings us to God; He gives us a new birth into a living hope and an inheritance; He is always the same.) **Which one of these verses is special to you? Why?** (Allow response.) **Encourage pupils to think about personal reasons Jesus is a special gift.**

5 Personal Praise

Pupils will prepare role plays about ways a person can give of himself or herself. Provide copies of Activity Page 4C and pencils. Divide this group into three small ones. Assign one situation to each group. Each group is to come up with a solution and prepare the role play. If your group is too small for this, allow the group to work together on the endings for all the situations, then choose the one they like best to role play. Have the instructions taped or written ahead of time.

Instruct the pupils to read the situations given on the activity page. Pupils are to finish the stories to show how the characters can give of themselves. During *Sharing in Worship*, the pupils will act out the situations to show the others how a person can give of himself or herself.

God gave us the gift of His Son, Jesus. We can praise and glorify God by thanking Him for this gift. One way we can do this is by giving something back to God. How can we do that? (Allow response.) **Using our time, our money, our talents, our influence for God are all ways we can give something back to God. When we do what God wants us to do we are giving something of ourselves to God. We are showing our thankfulness for what He has given us. We are praising God, or telling Him He is important and special when we choose to do what He wants us to do.**

How could Matthew give of himself? (Give God his time by shoveling the sidewalk of the elderly man.) **How could Kara give of herself?** (Keep her commitment and wrap presents.) **How could Michael give of himself?** (By giving part or all of the money to the missionary and waiting longer to buy the bike.) **What are some ways you can give of yourself?** (Allow response.)

6 Prayer

Pupils will write a prayer-poem to thank and/or praise God for the gift of His Son. Pupils will need poster board, markers, paper, and pencils. Write "Jesus Is God's Gift to Me" on the top of the poster board.

Have the pupils brainstorm reasons why Jesus is a special gift. (You may choose to provide the Scriptures given on Activity Page 4B if the pupils need help.) After the pupils have compiled a list, have them write a prayer/poem to be read during *Sharing in Worship*. The prayer/poem should praise or thank God for the special gift of His Son. The poem should also include reasons why Jesus is a special gift. This can be a free verse poem; it does not need to rhyme.

Sharing in Worship

20-25 minutes

Call to Worship

Group 1 created a collage showing ways they can praise God for the gift of His Son. Have a pupil read Luke 2:13, 14, and

20. Then have pupils display their collage and offer any explanations that are needed.

Devotion

Group 2 will tell us our Scripture story and use dioramas they made as visuals. Have children tell the account of Luke 2:1-20 showing their dioramas.

The birth of Jesus was no ordinary event. His birth was prophesied, or foretold, many years earlier. Angels appeared and praised God for the birth of Jesus. When the shepherds saw Jesus they glorified and praised God for Jesus. Jesus was a very special baby because He is God's Son. God sent Him to earth for a specific purpose, and that was so He could die for our sins. God gave us His Son as a gift, so that we could have our sins forgiven and be able to spend eternity with God. Jesus was the most special gift you or I could ever receive. We can praise God, just as the angels and shepherds did for the gift of His Son, Jesus.

Music

Have the pupils in Group 3 lead the singing of the four Christmas songs they have on their activity page.

Scripture

Group 4 did research to find things about Jesus that make Him a special gift. Have each pupil read a verse and then tell why Jesus is a special gift.

Lord's Supper

Jesus is a special gift to us because it is only through His death that we can be forgiven of our sins and be able to come to God. As we take the Lord's Supper, we should remember that Jesus' blood was shed to give us the precious gift of forgiveness of sins and eternal life.

Offering

God gave us a very special gift when He sent His Son, Jesus, to this earth. We can thank Him by the giving of ourselves and our money. As you give your gift to God today, remember the special gift of His Son.

Personal Praise

Group 5 will do three short skits showing how they can give of themselves to God.

Prayer

Have the pupils read aloud in unison the poem they wrote.

Closing Moments

10-15 minutes

Christmas Bookmarks. Provide construction paper, Christmas seals, markers, glue, scissors, and so on. Have the children make bookmarks that tell about God's gift of His Son, Jesus. The pupils may use these as Christmas gifts.

Songs and Scriptures

Look up the Scriptures and think about the words of the songs listed. Draw a line from each song to the Scripture reference from which the song came. Practice singing the songs so you can lead them during worship.

Philippians 2:9-11 Luke 2:10-14 Micah 5:a, 4, 5 Luke 2:6, 7

© 1994 by The STANDARD PUBLISHING COMPANY. Permission is granted to photocopy this page for ministry purposes only—not for resale.

4A

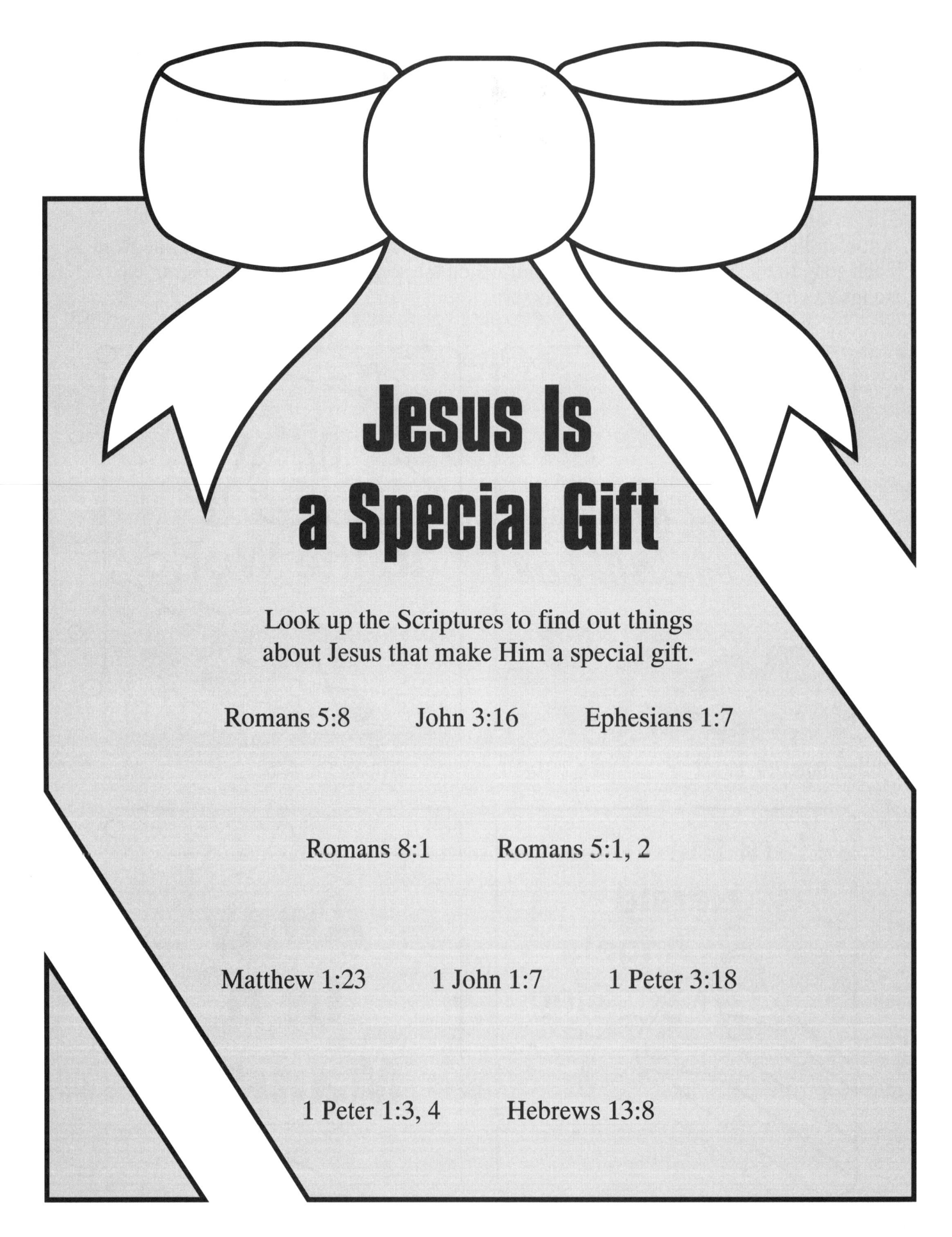

Jesus Is a Special Gift

Look up the Scriptures to find out things about Jesus that make Him a special gift.

Romans 5:8   John 3:16   Ephesians 1:7

Romans 8:1   Romans 5:1, 2

Matthew 1:23   1 John 1:7   1 Peter 3:18

1 Peter 1:3, 4   Hebrews 13:8

Giving Myself to God

Read the situations. Make up an ending for each story showing how the person could give of himself. Practice acting out the stories to present during worship.

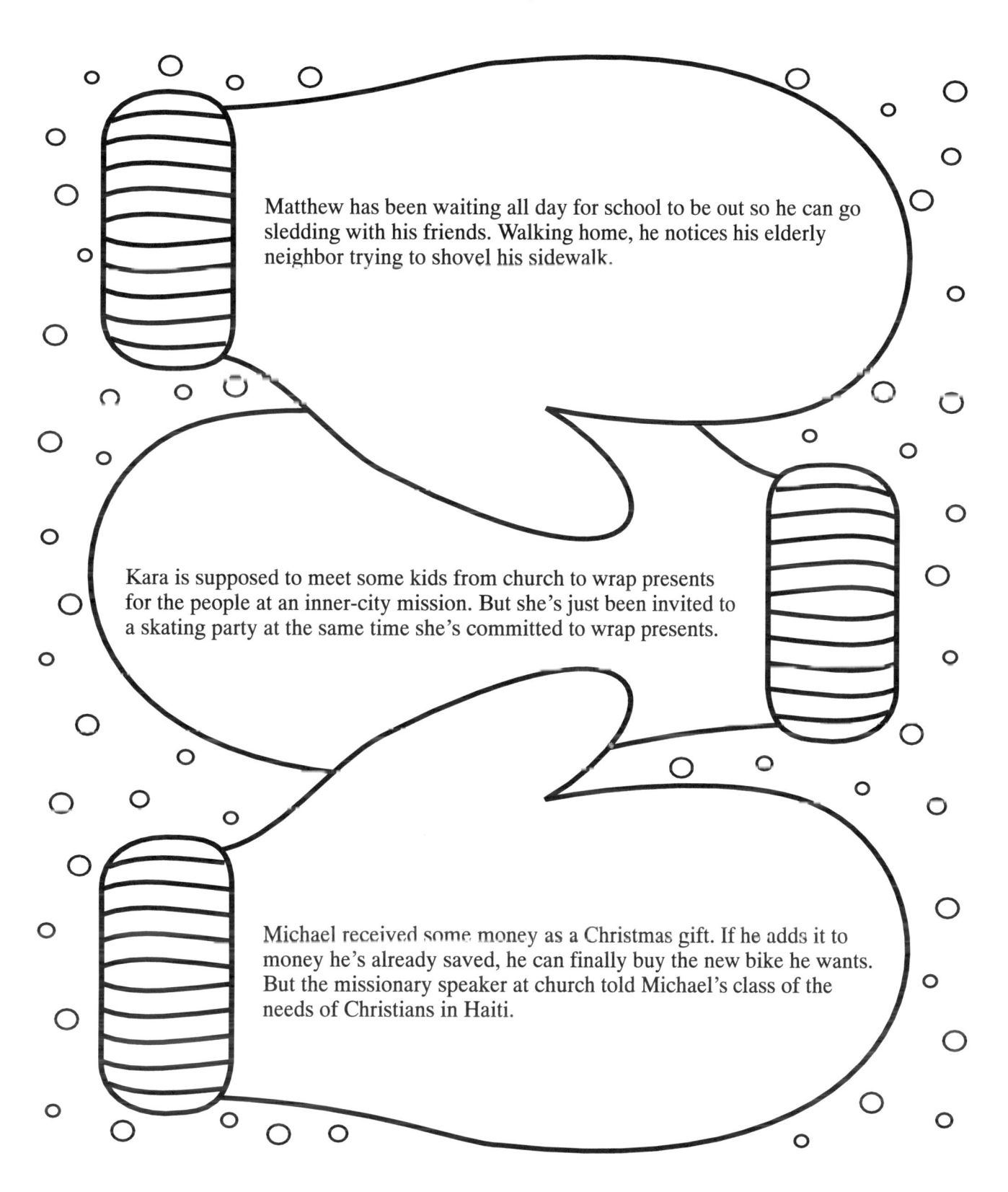

Matthew has been waiting all day for school to be out so he can go sledding with his friends. Walking home, he notices his elderly neighbor trying to shovel his sidewalk.

Kara is supposed to meet some kids from church to wrap presents for the people at an inner-city mission. But she's just been invited to a skating party at the same time she's committed to wrap presents.

Michael received some money as a Christmas gift. If he adds it to money he's already saved, he can finally buy the new bike he wants. But the missionary speaker at church told Michael's class of the needs of Christians in Haiti.

© 1994 by The STANDARD PUBLISHING COMPANY. Permission is granted to photocopy this page for ministry purposes only—not for resale.

4C

Bible Story: God Protects His Son
Matthew 2:1, 2, 11-23

Unit 1: Trust God Who Keeps His Promises
Session 5

Worship Focus: Worship God because He protects those who trust Him.

An Escape to Egypt

Transition Time
10-15 minutes

Send the pupils in small groups to the rest rooms and drinking fountain. Welcome newcomers and involve everyone in the following activity.

Danger! Danger! Before class write each of the following on a separate index card: smoke alarm, fire injury, insect repellent, bug bites, goggles, eye injury, shots, disease, life jacket, drowning, sunscreen, sunburn, bike helmet, head injury, child-proof lids, accidental poisoning. You may prepare additional index cards if you have a large group. Each child should receive one index card. Explain to the pupils that each has a word that protects people from something or a word that tells something from which people need protection. At a given signal, pupils will pair up with their appropriate partners. If the pupils accomplish this quickly, shuffle the cards and repeat the activity.

Launching the Theme
10 minutes

Why do we need protection from the things that are written on these cards? (Allow response.) **Yes, without protection we can be seriously injured or get very sick. In some circumstances, we could even die without the proper protection. What other things can you think of from which you need protection?** (Allow response.)

In our lesson today, we see how young Jesus needed protection. King Herod was searching for Jesus so he could kill Him. In a dream, an angel from God told Joseph what to do to protect little Jesus. Joseph knew God's wisdom was perfect and he trusted God to care for Jesus. Joseph obeyed God's instructions and Jesus was kept safe.

God loves us very much and has promised to protect us. We don't need to fear with God as our protector. Today we will worship God because He protects those who trust Him.

Briefly explain the choices of preparation for worship. Allow the children to choose the groups in which they would like to participate.

Building the Theme
30 minutes

E easy   **I** independent   **A** advanced

1 Call to Worship **A**
Pupils will prepare a choral reading

about God's protection. For this activity pupils will need Bibles, copies of Activity Page 5A, and pencils.

Have the pupils begin by looking up and reading Psalm 121. The pupils will create a choral reading using verses from this psalm and other lines they write describing times when God protects them. During *Sharing in Worship,* the group will present the choral reading aloud.

According to this psalm, who protects us? (The Lord.) **What phrase describes how He protects?** (He will not let your foot slip. He does not slumber or sleep. He watches over you. He keeps you from all harm.) **What kind of protection do you need?** (Allow response.) **We need protection from sin, from Satan, or from people who would harm us. If we stop and pray when we are tempted to sin, God will protect us by giving us strength to say no to the temptation. Sometimes we need physical protection from people or things that threaten us, and sometimes we need to be protected from the consequences of our foolish activities or decisions.**

2 Scripture

Pupils will learn more about God's protection as they solve a puzzle. They will need copies of Activity Page 5B, pencils, and Bibles. Pupils will share their information about God's protection just after the Call to Worship.

Have the pupils look up the verses. **Who does God protect?** (His faithful ones; the simple hearted; he who acknowledges God's name.) **From what does God protect His people?** (He protects from the evil one [Satan], from trouble, from men of violence.) **Does this mean you will never have to face these problems?** (No, but God is with me and in control of the situation. He knows what is best for me.) **Can you think of some Bible people who were protected by God?** (Help pupils recall people such as Noah, Moses, Peter, and Paul.)

3 Devotion E

Pupils will prepare a TV program of the Bible story. This activity will require Bibles, a corrugated cardboard box, a roll of large paper such as newsprint or shelf paper, markers or crayons, and scissors. Ahead of time, cut a large opening in the front of the box for a TV "screen." Then cut slits on both sides of the box long enough to accommodate the width of the paper you will be using. Pupils will thread their paper roll through the first slit, past the "screen," and out the second slit. When the program is presented, the pupils will slowly pull the paper through, from scene to scene, as someone narrates or explains the scenes. Make sure there is about 2 feet of blank paper before the first scene begins.

Have the pupils read Matthew 2:1, 2, 11-23. After they have read the account, help them decide on what scenes are necessary, and then begin their illustrations of the Scriptures in chronological order. After all the scenes have been completed, help the pupils feed the paper roll through the slits of the TV. During *Sharing in Worship,* the pupils will feed the paper roll through, showing one scene at a time and explaining the illustration.

Who heard the king of the Jews had been born? (Magi from the east.) **What did the Magi do when they arrived at the house where Jesus was?** (They bowed and worshiped Him. They brought Him expensive gifts of gold.) **What message did an angel give Joseph after the Magi left?** (To take Jesus and Mary to Egypt.) **Why was Jesus in danger?** (King Herod wanted Jesus dead because He was a threat to Herod.) **How long did Jesus stay in Egypt?** (Until Herod died.) **Then what message was Joseph given?** (To take Jesus and Mary to Israel because Herod was dead.) **Where did Jesus live?** (Nazareth.) **Was Jesus protected?** (Yes.)

4 Music

Pupils will describe and illustrate God's protection through music and art. Pupils will need paper, markers or crayons, and Bibles.

To start, ask pupils to look up and read Psalm 5:11 ("But let all who take refuge in you be glad; let them ever sing for joy. Spread your protection over them, that those who love your name may rejoice in you"); and Psalm 32:7 ("You are my hiding place; you will protect me from trouble and surround me with songs of deliverance"). Then have pupils write a song about God's protection to the tune of "Father, I Adore You." The first line could be, "God will protect me." The other lines could be about how God protects those who trust Him. After the song is ready, pupils can use the markers or crayons to draw illustrations of ways God protects them. If your group is large, have half work on the song while the other half illustrates God's protection. During *Sharing in Worship*, the pupils will sing their new song as they display their illustrations.

What do these verses tell you about God's protection? (I can be happy [joyful] because of God's protection. God is a "hiding place" where I can go for protection from trouble. I am surrounded with songs of deliverance.) **How do you get God's protection?** (Through prayer, reading the Bible, listening to parents and others who can help you.)

5 Personal Praise

Each pupil will write a story about a time when God protected him or her. Pupils will need copies of Activity Page 5C, and pencils or pens.

Try to think of a time when God protected you. Perhaps it was a time when you narrowly missed being in an automobile accident. Maybe the school bully threatened you and God kept you from getting hurt. Or, perhaps God protected you and your family from a flood, a fire, or an earthquake. Perhaps God used a person—a parent or teacher, a fire fighter or police officer—to save you from something. As you think of ways God has protected you, fill in the blanks on the activity page to write a story that you will read during *Sharing in Worship*.

6 Prayer

Pupils will make cards to say thank-you to God for His protection. This activity will require construction paper, markers, scissors, glue, glitter, yarn, fabric scraps, and pens. If you need to save time in class, cut sheets of construction paper in half and fold to make the cards ahead of time. Write or tape brief instructions if this is to be used as an independent activity.

Pupils may decorate the cards any way they wish. Each pupil should write a short prayer inside the card. During *Sharing in Worship*, the pupils will show their cards and read their prayers aloud.

Does God protect you? Why? (Allow response. God protects me because He loves me and I trust Him to protect me.) **Does that mean that God will never let anything bad happen to you?** (No. He has promised to help me handle difficult or dangerous situations.) **Are you glad God protects you? Why?** (Allow response. When God protects me, I don't need to fear because God is greater than anyone or anything.) **How can you thank God for His protection?** (By telling Him.)

Sharing in Worship

20-25 minutes

If you did not have pupils do all the activities, plan to present them yourself or have another adult or two help you. Omit any activity that is too involved for you to do without help from the group.

Call to Worship
Group 1 prepared a choral reading about God's protection. Have the group present their choral reading.

Scripture
Group 2 discovered what the Bible says about God's protection. They will read their verses at this time.

Devotion
Group 3 will present their TV story of today's lesson. Have the pupils roll the paper past the "screen" and tell the story from Matthew 2:1, 2, 11-23.

How did God protect Jesus? (Allow response.) **God warned Joseph to take Jesus to a safer place when He was in danger. Why do you think God protected Jesus?** (Allow response.) **God loved Jesus and wanted to protect Him from being killed. Does God love you?** (Yes.) **Do you think God wants to protect you?** (Yes.) **From what kinds of things does God protect you?** (Allow response.) **Throughout history we can see times when God protected His people from other nations. We can see how God protected people such as baby Moses, Noah, and David. God's Word tells us He is faithful and will protect us from the evil one. Even when it may seem hard to trust God, we know He will protect us. God hasn't promised us that nothing bad will happen to us. He has, however, promised to help us face whatever problems or difficult situations may come to us. We know our lives are in God's hands. He loves us and cares for us.**

Music
Group 4 wrote a song about God's protection. They have also illustrated ways God protects them. Have the pupils take turns sharing their illustrations. Then have them sing their song as special music.

Personal Praise
Members of Group 5 also know firsthand about God's protection. They will read stories about times God protected them.

Lord's Supper
God protected us from having to spend eternity separated from Him. He sent Jesus to die on the cross so we would not have to spend eternity in Hell because of our sins. As we take the Lord's Supper, let's remember that God protected us by sending Jesus to die for us.

Offering
Let's give our offerings as a way to say thank-you to God for His protection.

Prayer
Group 6 made cards to express thanks to God for His protection. Have the pupils display their cards and read their prayers aloud.

Closing Moments
10-15 minutes

Nature's Protection. Have the pupils think of ways animals protect themselves. (Remind the pupils that God created animals with these ways to protect themselves.) See how many different animals and methods of protection pupils can think of. Make a list of these on the chalkboard or on a poster board. (For example: porcupine—quills; birds—camouflage; deer—speed; rabbit—color of fur; some butterflies—bitter taste; rhinoceros—horns on nose; ostrich—speed; turtle—shell; kangaroo—pouch for baby; camel—can go for long time without water; giraffe—tall, good eyesight, and so on.) If you want to make this a game, divide the group into two teams. Teams will take turns naming animals and their protection until one team runs out of ideas.

God Will Protect

Write lines to complete the choral reading. Every other line is provided for you. Write about times when God protects you—from sin, from Satan, or from people or things that would harm you.

Speaker 1: I will lift up my eyes to the hills—where does my help come from?
My help comes from the Lord, the Maker of heaven and earth.

Speaker 2: _____
_____
_____

Speaker 1: He will not let your foot slip—he who watches over you will not slumber;
indeed, he who watches over Israel will neither slumber nor sleep.

Speaker 3: _____
_____
_____

Speaker 1: The Lord watches over you—the Lord is your shade at your right hand.
The sun will not harm you by day, nor the moon by night.

Speaker 4: _____
_____
_____

Speaker 1: The Lord will keep you from all harm—he will watch over your life;
the Lord will watch over your coming and going both now and forevermore (Psalm 121).

5A © 1994 by The STANDARD PUBLISHING COMPANY. Permission is granted to photocopy this page for ministry purposes only—not for resale.

The Key 15

Fifteen key words have been left out of these verses. Look up the Scriptures to find out what God's Word says about His protection, and fill in the fifteen key words.

2 Thessalonians 3:3—The Lord is ①_____, and he will ②_____ and ③_____ you from the evil ④_____.

John 17:11, 12—Jesus asked God to ③_____ His disciples—"so they may be ④_____ as we are ④_____."

Psalm 37:28—The Lord ⑤_____s the ⑥_____, and he will not ⑦_____ his ①_____ ④_____s. They will be ③_____ed forever.

Psalm 116:6—The Lord ③_____s the ⑧_____.

Proverbs 2:8—He ⑨_____ the course of the ⑥_____ and ③_____s the way of his ①_____ ④_____s.

Psalm 32:7—You are my ⑩_____ place; you will ③_____ me from ⑪_____.

Psalm 40:11—May your ⑤_____ and your ⑫_____ always ③_____ me.

Psalm 91:14—Because he ⑤_____s me, says the Lord, I will ⑬_____ him; I will ③_____ him, for he acknowledges my ⑭_____.

Psalm 140:1—⑬_____ me, O Lord, from evil ⑮_____; ③_____ me from ⑮_____ of violence.

© 1994 by The STANDARD PUBLISHING COMPANY. Permission is granted to photocopy this page for ministry purposes only—not for resale.

Write a Story

Use the ideas below to write a story about ways God has protected you.

I'm glad God protects me. I remember once when _____
describe a time when you were in danger or were tempted to sin

_____;

God really helped me then!

Another time He used _____ to
name a person or a title (such as police officer or fire fighter)

protect me from _____
dangerous situation

_____. I could have _____

_____,
consequences of the situation

but God spared me!

Sometimes now I'm tempted to be afraid of _____
describe something you're afraid of

_____.

But I know God will protect me, because He tells me in His Word _____

_____.
quote or paraphrase a verse from the Bible that tells about God's protection

5C © 1994 by The STANDARD PUBLISHING COMPANY. Permission is granted to photocopy this page for ministry purposes only—not for resale.

Bible Story: Pray for Wisdom to Please God
Luke 2:40-52

Unit 2: God Answers When We Pray
Session 6

Worship Focus: Worship God because He is wise.

The Wise One

Transition Time
10-15 minutes

Send the children in small groups to the rest rooms and drinking fountain. Then begin the following activity.

Wise Moves. Before class, print the four letters of the word *wise* separately on sheets of paper. Choose four children to sit in front of the room and give them each a letter in this order: E, I, S, W. **With these letters, you need to spell a word by telling two people sitting next to each other to trade places. Make good choices because you need to spell the word by switching couples five or less times. Remember, only people sitting next to each other can trade.**

Let a volunteer suggest which of the four children should trade places first. If the class agrees, instruct the pair to trade. If WISE is not spelled in five moves or less, place the four students back in their original order and have the class try again. When WISE is spelled, repeat with four new children in a different order.

Launching the Theme
10 minutes

You had to consider possible moves before you could spell WISE. Do you think your moves were wise? (Allow responses.) **What is wisdom?** (Write the pupils' definitions on the chalkboard.)

Have a student read James 3:13. **Wisdom is more than just knowing things. It also involves using what you know. You have to use knowledge and understanding to make good and right decisions. Today we will focus on God's wisdom. We will worship God because He is wise.**

Building the Theme
30 minutes

E easy   **I** independent   **A** advanced

1 Call to Worship
Pupils will illustrate words describing God's wisdom. Provide *ICB, NIV, KJV* and *TLB* versions of the Bible, a dictionary, white construction paper, pencils, crayons or markers, a chalkboard, and chalk.

Have pupils read Job 9:4 in an *ICB*: "God's wisdom is deep, and his power is great." **What word describes God's wisdom?** (Deep.) Write "deep" on the chalkboard. **What other things are deep?** (Allow responses.) **How can a seed in the ground and an ocean with a bottom miles from the surface both be called**

43

deep? (Deep is relative to what it describes.) **We know God is the powerful creator of the universe. So, what does deep say about God's wisdom?** (Great, vast.) **Let's see what words other Bible versions use to describe God's wisdom.** Have pupils read Job 9:4 in the other Bible versions and write the words or phrases on the chalkboard that describe God's wisdom. (Profound; wise in heart; so wise.) Have pupils look up unfamiliar words in the dictionary and add their meanings to the chalkboard. **Although these versions use different words, they all say that God is very wise.**

Give each pupil a word from the chalkboard to illustrate on construction paper. Under their pictures, pupils will complete the sentence, "God's wisdom is _____ ." The drawings will be shown and sentences read during *Sharing in Worship*. Pupils who are uncomfortable showing their illustrations may prefer to explain their sentences.

2 Music

Pupils will write and prepare songs for worship. Provide Bibles, hymn or praise chorus books for unfamiliar songs, two large sheets of construction paper, adding machine tape or paper strips, a stapler, and markers.

Read Daniel 2:20. **We are going to prepare songs today to praise God for His wisdom.** First, have pupils change "Rain, Rain, Go Away," to "Wise, Wise, God Is Wise." Have them write on paper strips several ideas for the song's second line such as, "Worship Him every day," or, "Sing His praises every day." Staple the strips to construction paper. Sing "Wise, wise, God is wise," before each paper-strip sentence.

Help the group choose other songs concerning God's wisdom for worship. Use your own or the following: "Praise the Lord Together Singing" (changing the second line to "He is so wise"); "Heavenly Father, I Appreciate You"; "Be Still and Know"; and "Thou Art Worthy." Let volunteers write the song titles on construction paper to display for worship.

3 Devotion A

Pupils will complete an activity page and write a verse in the form of an eye chart. Provide Bibles, copies of Activity Page 6A, pencils, white construction paper, and markers.

Read 1 Corinthians 1:24. What does this verse say about God's wisdom? (Christ is the wisdom of God.) This is a difficult concept. You may want to refer to Colossians 2:2, 3 and 1 Corinthians 1:30. **Today's activity page will help you understand this verse.** (The answer is: We see God's wisdom through Jesus.) On the back of the activity page, have pupils list some things Jesus did that show God's wisdom, such as, "told parables" and "died on the cross." Print a composite list on construction paper. Have pupils individually write 1 Corinthians 1:24 in the form of an eye chart.

For *Sharing in Worship*, pupils will read together 1 Corinthians 1:24 from their charts and a volunteer will read an explanation of this verse from the activity page. Others will read some things Jesus did that show God's wisdom.

4 Offering E

Pupils will create a collage showing God's wisdom in creation. Provide Bibles, magazines, poster board, scissors, glue, and markers.

Have pupils summarize Psalm 104:24 and Proverbs 3:19, 20. **We see God's wisdom in His creation.** Let a volunteer write Psalm 104:24 on the poster, leaving room for pictures.

From Job 38 and 39, divide the following verses among the pupils. Help them determine what matching pictures they should find to glue on the poster: 38:4-6 (earth); 8-11 (sea and clouds); 12 (sun); 22-30 (weather); 36 (people); 38:39; 39:1, 19, 26, 27 (animals).

The group will show its collage before the Offering. A volunteer will read Psalm 104:24.

If there is time, play "I Spy," naming things God created.

5 Scripture

Pupils will prepare illustrations contrasting God's wisdom to man's. Provide Bibles and a variety of objects, such as marshmallows, jars, paper, markers, ribbon, yarn, a flashlight, sand, graph paper, or other items of your choosing.

Draw a line down the middle of the chalkboard. On the left side, write the word *wise*. **What is the opposite of wise?** (Write the group's response on the right.) Continue by writing the words *big, great, deep,* and *complete* on the left and the opposites given by the pupils on the right. When this is finished, write "God's Wisdom" as a title over the left side and "Man's Wisdom" as a title over the right side. **The Bible tells us that God's wisdom is much greater than any wisdom people have. The words on the left can describe God's wisdom. Our wisdom is very small compared to God's!**

Ask a pupil to read 1 Corinthians 1:25. **This verse does not mean that God is foolish or has any foolishness in Him. It is showing us how much greater God's wisdom is than ours.** Have pupils explain the following verses: Proverbs 3:7; 21:30; Isaiah 55:8, 9; Romans 11:33. **These verses tell us we can't even compare with God's wisdom. We can't count on our wisdom, so we need to turn to God for direction.**

Divide the group in pairs. Have each pair use the material you provided to develop an illustration of the difference between God's wisdom and man's wisdom. For example, pupils could make a small dot for man's wisdom on a large piece of paper representing God's wisdom. They could fill a jar with white marshmallows for God's wisdom and include one pink one for man's wisdom.

Pupils could compare the sun to a flashlight, a grain of sand to a pile of sand, one snowflake to a mountain of snow, etc.

For *Sharing in Worship*, a volunteer will read 1 Corinthians 1:25 and pupils will explain their depictions of God's wisdom.

6 Prayer

Pupils will prepare a responsive reading for the closing prayer. Provide Bibles, paper, poster board or construction paper, markers, and pencils. If pupils will be working on their own, tape or write instructions for them.

There are many verses in the Bible that praise God. We will look at some verses that praise God for His wisdom. Read Romans 11:33-36; 16:27; and Revelation 7:12.

A doxology is a praise to God. You will write your own question/answer doxology based on the verses we just read. You will write a total of twelve questions and their answers, two for each verse. For example, using Romans 11:33, pupils could write, "Whose wisdom has no end? God's wisdom!" Read one verse at a time and ask a volunteer to record suggestions on paper. Group members will write the final copy on poster board or construction paper.

During *Sharing in Worship*, pupils from Group 6 will read the questions and the large group will read the answers.

Sharing in Worship

20-25 minutes

If you did not have pupils do all the activities, plan to present them yourself or have another adult or two help you. Omit any activity that is too involved for you to do without help from the group.

Call to Worship

Today we are worshiping God because He is wise. Group 1 read Job 9:4 in sev-

eral Bible versions to find words describing God's wisdom. Pupils read their sentences and show their pictures.

Music
With music we can praise God for His wisdom. Group 2 will lead the songs.

Devotion
Before the session, write "God's wisdom" on white poster board with white crayon. Have a dark marker available.

We can see God's wisdom through His Son, Jesus. Group 3 will read some things Jesus did that show God's wisdom. Group 3 reads from the list.

Even when Jesus was twelve, He was wise. Jesus' parents took Him to the Passover Feast in Jerusalem. On the way home, they realized that Jesus was not with their group. After much searching, they found Him in the temple, discussing God's Word with the religious teachers and surprising them with His wisdom. As Jesus grew older, His wisdom increased and God was pleased with Him.

How did Jesus' death show God's wisdom? (Allow responses.) **God didn't want our sin to separate us from Him; so He sent Jesus to save us. Jesus died on the cross, taking the punishment for our sin. We can't touch wisdom, but we can see it in what God did and through Jesus, His Son. We can't appreciate God's wisdom without knowing Jesus.**

This marker represents Jesus. As the pupils watch, use the marker to shade over the crayon words. The words will become visible. **Jesus helps us see God's wisdom more clearly.** Group 3 reads and explains 1 Corinthians 1:24.

Lord's Supper
The Lord's Supper is a special time to remember that God, in His great wisdom, sent Jesus to die for us. Jesus took our sins on himself. Use the quiet time now to think about Jesus and tell God how grateful you are. Think also about what you have been doing this week to show your gratitude. Ask forgiveness for any unloving things you did.

Offering
Group 4 made a poster showing God's creation. The group displays the collage and reads the verse. **God created everything. It all belongs to Him. Let's give back to Him some of the money He has allowed us to have.**

Scripture
This group has some interesting illustrations comparing God's wisdom to man's wisdom. Group 5 first reads the Scripture and then shows what they prepared.

Prayer
For a closing prayer, Group 6 wrote a responsive praise to God. They will read the questions, and you will read the answers. Think about the words as you read.

Closing Moments
10-15 minutes

Words of Wisdom. Distribute copies of Activity Page 6B and pencils. Have pupils complete the page to review Scriptures on wisdom. The verses are taken from the *ICB* version.

Read 1 Corinthians 1:24. Follow the clues to reveal a message in the eye chart.

How's Your Vision?

W

PEABKQVCNOLFX
VBDCQGYZFXKAP
YZKHNFBPHQCDL
CQPAGNKOBFLVY
FYCBUIALVKZXQ
BPLKYZJEFCANV
XBACNVZMYBEKP
FZYBSQXNOCACL
SCFAVEPKZSNXB
KAQBNVXYNSRZC
CBAWZKQLVXYTN
ACLZPYSAFZBXU

- Circle the W in row 1, the second letter in row 2, the third letter in row 3, and so on.
- Circle those same letters again wherever you find them on the eye chart.
- Unscramble the circled letters on the lines below. The number under each line refers to the row the letter is found in. Each letter is used once.

__ __ __ __ __ __ __ __ , __ __ __ __ __ __
1 2 10 7 8 5 5 4   9 12 6 10 3 9 8

__ __ __ __ __ __ __ __ __ __ __
12 4 11 2 13 3 4   7 10 11 6 13

© 1994 by The STANDARD PUBLISHING COMPANY. Permission is granted to photocopy this page for ministry purposes only—not for resale.

6A

James 3:13 — __ __ th __ r __ anyon __ among you who __ __ truly w __ __ __ an __ un __ __ r __ tan __ ng? Th __ n h __ __ h o u l __ __ how h __ __ w __ __ __ om by l __ v __ ng r __ ght.

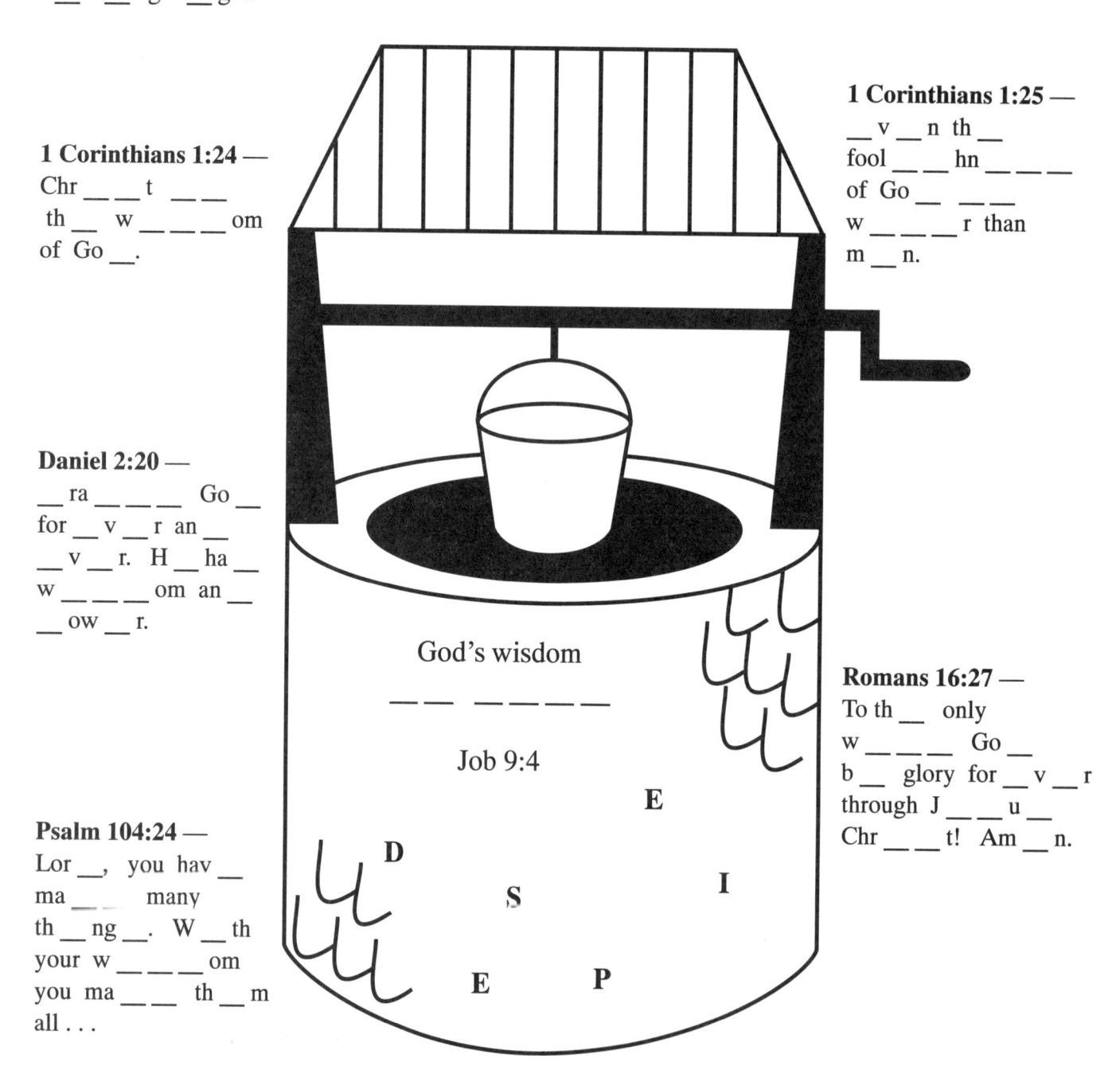

1 Corinthians 1:24 — Chr __ __ __ t __ __ __ th __ w __ __ __ om of Go __.

1 Corinthians 1:25 — __ v __ n th __ fool __ __ hn __ __ __ __ of Go __ __ __ w __ __ __ r than m __ n.

Daniel 2:20 — __ ra __ __ __ __ __ Go __ for __ v __ r an __ __ v __ r. H __ ha __ w __ __ __ __ om an __ __ ow __ r.

God's wisdom

__ __ __ __ __ __ __

Job 9:4

E
D
S   I
E   P

Romans 16:27 — To th __ only w __ __ __ __ Go __ b __ glory for __ v __ r through J __ __ u __ Chr __ __ t! Am __ n.

Psalm 104:24 — Lor __, you hav __ ma __ __ many th __ ng __. W __ th your w __ __ __ om you ma __ __ th __ m all . . .

Words of Wisdom

Read Job 9:4 and unscramble the letters on the well to describe God's wisdom.
Then put those letters in the blanks to complete the other verses.

6B   © 1994 by The STANDARD PUBLISHING COMPANY. Permission is granted to photocopy this page for ministry purposes only—not for resale.

Bible Story: Pray for Courage to Repent
Luke 3:2, 3, 10-16, 18

Unit 2: God Answers When We Pray
Session 7

Worship Focus: Worship God because He forgives us.

God's Great Forgiveness

Transition Time

10-15 minutes

Send the children in small groups to the rest rooms and water fountain. Set one less chair than the number of pupils in a circle facing outward; then begin the following game.

Chair Sitters. As in "Musical Chairs," pupils walk while the music plays and sit when it stops. In "Chair Sitters," however, chairs are not removed, but blocked. Each child left standing blocks one of the chairs for the rest of the game by sitting in it, keeping his or her feet under the chair. Repeat until one child is left.

Launching the Theme

10 minutes

Have available a bowl of water, matches, and a small piece of soap. **In our game today, many of you blocked chairs to keep others out. What can block our way to God?** (Sin.) **We sin when we disobey God.**

Read Isaiah 59:2. **Sin separates us from God. Pretend we are like matches that are close to God when centered in this bowl.** Float a few matches in the middle of the bowl. **This soap represents sin.** Have the class watch you place a piece of soap near the matches. The matches will move away. **Sin separates us from God, but because God loves us, He made a way to forgive sin.** Remove the soap and place the matches back in the center. **God's forgiveness lets us be close to Him. Today we are worshiping God because He forgives us.**

Building the Theme

30 minutes

E easy   **I** independent   **A** advanced

1 Call to Worship [E]

Pupils will write sins on cards and memorize a verse about God's forgiveness. You will need Bibles, index cards, chalkboard and chalk, and pencils. Beforehand, write the fourteen letters of "God forgives sin," separately on cards.

The Bible says we all sin. Read 1 John 1:8 with the group. **In what ways do you sin?** (Allow responses.) Have pupils write one sin on each of fourteen blank cards.

When we repent, we are sorry for our sins and try to do right. There is good news for those who repent. Ask a pupil to read Psalm 65:3 for the group to repeat. (The *International Children's Bible* would be easiest for children to use here.) Help pupils compare Psalm 65:3 with Micah

49

7:18; Psalm 130:3, 4, and Daniel 9:9.

Shuffle the sin and letter cards together, laying them face down. **We are going to play "Hangman."** Draw a noose on the chalkboard. **I will call one of you to pick a card. If it has a letter on it, everyone will say Psalm 65:3 together. If it names a sin, I will add a body part to the noose because sin can destroy people. Work together to collect fourteen letters before getting hung; then unscramble their message.** Play the game, drawing fourteen body parts, such as a head, body, arms, legs, eyes, nose, mouth, hands, and feet.

For *Sharing in Worship*, the group will read their sin cards and recite Psalm 65:3.

2 Scripture

Pupils will read and illustrate verses about God's forgiveness. Provide Bibles, copies of Activity Page 7A, pencils, and crayons. Tape or write out brief instructions for the pupils to follow.

There are many Bible verses that tell about God's great forgiveness. Distribute the activity page. The Scriptures are taken from the *ICB* version. (The missing words in order are: *east, west, covered, wipe out, threw, far away, swept away, big cloud, cloud, wash away, throw away, deepest sea,* and *remember*.) Have pupils share their responses to the activity at the bottom of the page. Assign a verse for each pupil to read during *Sharing in Worship*. Have each pupil illustrate his or her verse on the back of the page.

3 Music

Pupils will prepare songs for worship. Have Bibles, hymn or song books, mural paper, and markers (a tape player, and Scripture in song tape with a forgiveness song, optional).

God's forgiveness is an example for us to follow. Read Ephesians 4:32 and Colossians 3:13. **What do these verses tell us to do?** (Forgive each other.) If you are using a tape, play a forgiveness song for the group to learn and teach the class.

Next, have pupils use hymnals to find two or three songs about forgiveness, either God's forgiveness through Jesus or our forgiveness of each other. Possible songs are: "Freely, Freely"; "God Is So Good," adapting verses to tell of God's forgiveness; and "For God So Loved the World." Songs can be spoken as a rap if the music is unfamiliar. Have pupils practice their choices, write words or pictures to introduce the songs on mural paper, and decide who will lead each song for worship.

4 Devotion

Pupils will answer questions and complete an activity page. Provide Bibles, copies of Activity Page 7B, paper, and pencils.

I have two questions for you. Write each of the following questions and verses on paper. Choose pupils to add the group's answers. **The first question is, "What did the people in the Old Testament have to do to pay for their sins?" Use Leviticus 17:11 and Hebrews 9:22 for your answer.** (Blood of sacrifices was used to pay for sins temporarily. They had to be offered over and over.) **Let's read Hebrews 10:1b-4 and 11. Could the blood of animals take away sins?** (No.)

The second question is, "What took away the sins of people in the New Testament?" Use Hebrews 9:13, 14; 10:10, 12; and Ephesians 1:7. (Jesus' death paid for sin for all time and all people.)

The activity page has another verse about Jesus and forgiveness. Have pupils complete the page. (The answer is: "We owed a debt because we broke God's laws. That debt listed all the rules we failed to follow. But God forgave us that debt. He took away that debt and nailed it to the cross," Colossians 2:14, *ICB.*)

What question about the verse on your page can we ask the class? (Accept responses.) Have a pupil add the group's question and answer to the activity page.

Distribute the three questions to volunteers. For *Sharing in Worship*, each one will ask the class his or her question, wait for a response, and read one verse and the answer.

5 Lord's Supper

Pupils will write phrases from the activity page on paper hearts. Provide Bibles, copies of Activity Page 7C, pencils, paper, red construction paper, scissors, markers, and a dictionary.

If you eat too much, then what? (You gain weight.) **If you don't sleep, then . . .** (You are tired.) **If you don't eat your supper, then . . .** (You are hungry or miss dessert.) **There are consequences for our actions. If we sin, then what happens?** (We have a problem to deal with. We are sorry.) **Before God forgives, we need to do something.** Write on paper, "If we _____, then God forgives." **What do you think belongs in the blank?** (Allow responses.)

Work with pupils in completing the activity page. Then have each one cut a heart out of construction paper. Assign one true phrase and verse from the activity page for each pupil to write on his or her heart. Pupils will read their hearts before the Lord's Supper.

6 Prayer

Pupils will write poems for the closing prayer. Provide Bibles, paper, pencils, poster board, and markers. Before the session, write the following poem title and each of its lines on separate construction paper strips:

> **FORGIVE**
> Forgive me, God,
> Of all I've done.
> Remember not my sins.
> God, Your great forgiveness
> Is more than I deserve and
> Valued highly. Thank You for
> Extending forgiveness to me.

Display the strips randomly. **These are lines of a prayer-poem, but they are not in order. What line do you think belongs first?** Continue until the poem is unscrambled. **Does anyone see another word hidden in this poem?** (The first letter of each line spells the word forgive.) **This makes it an acrostic poem.**

There are three parts to this prayer-poem. The first three lines are similar to Psalm 25:11. What does the psalmist ask in this verse? (Asks God for forgiveness.) **Jesus gave an example of asking forgiveness.** Read Matthew 6:9-13.

The next two-and-one-half lines are similar to Psalm 86:5. What should we call this part? (Praising God for forgiveness.)

The end of the poem is similar to Psalm 136:1. Have a pupil read the verse. **What does this verse say to do?** (Thank God.)

When God forgives, our sins are gone. Divide the pupils into three groups to write acrostic prayer-poems, titled "GONE" or "AWAY." One group's poem will ask forgiveness, another group's poem will praise God, and the last group's will give thanks. The following is an example of being thankful:

> **GONE**
> God, You forgave
> Our sins. You will
> Never remember them
> Ever again. Thank You.

Have pupils write and illustrate their completed poems on poster board. These will be read at the end of the worship time.

Sharing in Worship

20-25 minutes

If you did not have pupils do all the activities, plan to present them yourself or have another adult or two help you. Omit any activity that is too involved for you to do without help from the group.

Call to Worship
We all sin, but we have a loving God who forgives when we repent. Group 1 will read examples of sin. After reading sin cards, pupils recite Psalm 65:3.

Scripture
Group 2 will read verses about God's great forgiveness. Pupils can also show their illustrations.

Music
God forgives us and wants us to forgive others. Group 3 will lead the forgiveness songs they prepared. Pupils use their mural to lead the songs.

Devotion
You will need one dirty penny for each child, a bowl with a mixture of 3 Tbs. vinegar and ½ tsp. salt, a second bowl of clean water, and a towel.

Group 4 has some questions for you. Students read their questions, call on pupils to respond, and read their answers with the supporting verse.

God used life-giving blood to take away sin. Before Jesus came, the people sacrificed animals repeatedly to roll back their sins. God provided a way to forgive sins once and for all when He sent Jesus to earth. God told John to prepare the people for Jesus. John preached about living right and repenting. Many of the people were sorry for the way they had lived and came to John to be baptized. Now we have forgiveness because Jesus' blood on the cross took away our sins forever. These dirty pennies are like our sin. Place a few pennies in the vinegar/salt solution briefly and rinse in clean water to show the sin is gone. The rest of the pennies will be cleaned during *Closing Moments*.

Lord's Supper
Group 5 will read what the Bible says we should do to be forgiven. Group 5 reads the words and Scriptures from their hearts. **If we are truly sorry and repent, we will do the things Group 5 read. We will ask for forgiveness and try to obey God. Quietly think about Jesus' death that gave us forgiveness, and pray that you will have a repentant heart.**

Offering
We can show our love and thanksgiving to God by giving to Him.

Prayer
Group 6 will read three prayer-poems they wrote. The first poem asks God for forgiveness. After this poem is read, pray silently, asking God to forgive your sins. One pupil reads the poem. **The next poem is a praise to God. Afterward, you will have time to praise God silently.** Allow time for the poem reading and prayer. **The last poem is a thanksgiving. Thank God quietly after you hear this poem.**

Closing Moments
10-15 minutes

As Clean As New. Help the children finish cleaning the pennies. To remain shiny, the pennies must be rinsed thoroughly in water. Each pupil will glue or tape a penny to an index card and add a sentence to remind him or her of the penny's significance, such as, "God sent Jesus to clean us of our sin." Pupils can decorate the cards with markers, yarn, ribbon, lace, or colorful self-adhesive plastic scraps.

God's Great Forgiveness

There are many verses in the Bible about God's great forgiveness. Here are some with missing words. What word or phrase do you think belongs in each blank? Choose words from Box A and write them in the MY GUESS column. Then check your guesses with the Scripture references from Box B and write the correct words in the BIBLE column. Write the missing Scripture references in the parentheses.

MY GUESS		BIBLE
1 _____	"He has taken our sins away from us as far as the __1__ is from the __2__." ( )	1 _____
2 _____		2 _____
3 _____	"You forgave the guilt of the people. You __3__ all their sins." ( )	3 _____
4 _____	"Turn your face from my sins. __4__ my guilt." ( )	4 _____
5 _____	"... You __5__ my sins __6__." ( )	5 _____
6 _____		6 _____
7 _____	"I have __7__ your sins like a __8__. I have removed your sins like a __9__ that disappears into the air. ..." ( )	7 _____
8 _____		8 _____
9 _____		9 _____
10 _____	"They sinned against me. But I will __10__ that sin. They did evil and turned away from me, but I will forgive them." ( )	10 _____
11 _____	"Lord, you will have mercy on us again. You will conquer our sins, you will __11__ all our sins into the __12__." ( )	11 _____
12 _____		12 _____
13 _____	"... I will forgive them for the wicked things they did, I will not __13__ their sins anymore." ( )	13 _____

A

east	cloud	threw
remember	west	wash away
throw away	swept away	covered
wipe out	big cloud	deepest sea
		far away

B

	Psalm 85:2	Jeremiah 33:8
Psalm 103:12	Micah 7:19	Psalm 51:9
Isaiah 38:17	Jeremiah 31:34	Isaiah 44:22

- Using a red crayon, circle three verses that say our sins are separated a great distance from us when we are forgiven.
- Using blue, circle five verses that use the word "away."
- With yellow, circle your favorite verse.
- With green, circle the two verses that use the word "guilt" when referring to sin.
- With purple, circle the verse that says something that God will not do.
  Some verses will be circled more than once.

© 1994 by The STANDARD PUBLISHING COMPANY. Permission is granted to photocopy this page for ministry purposes only—not for resale.

7A

Mystery Verse

Words of a Bible verse are written on these puzzle pieces. Match the puzzle pieces to the numbered spaces in the cross.

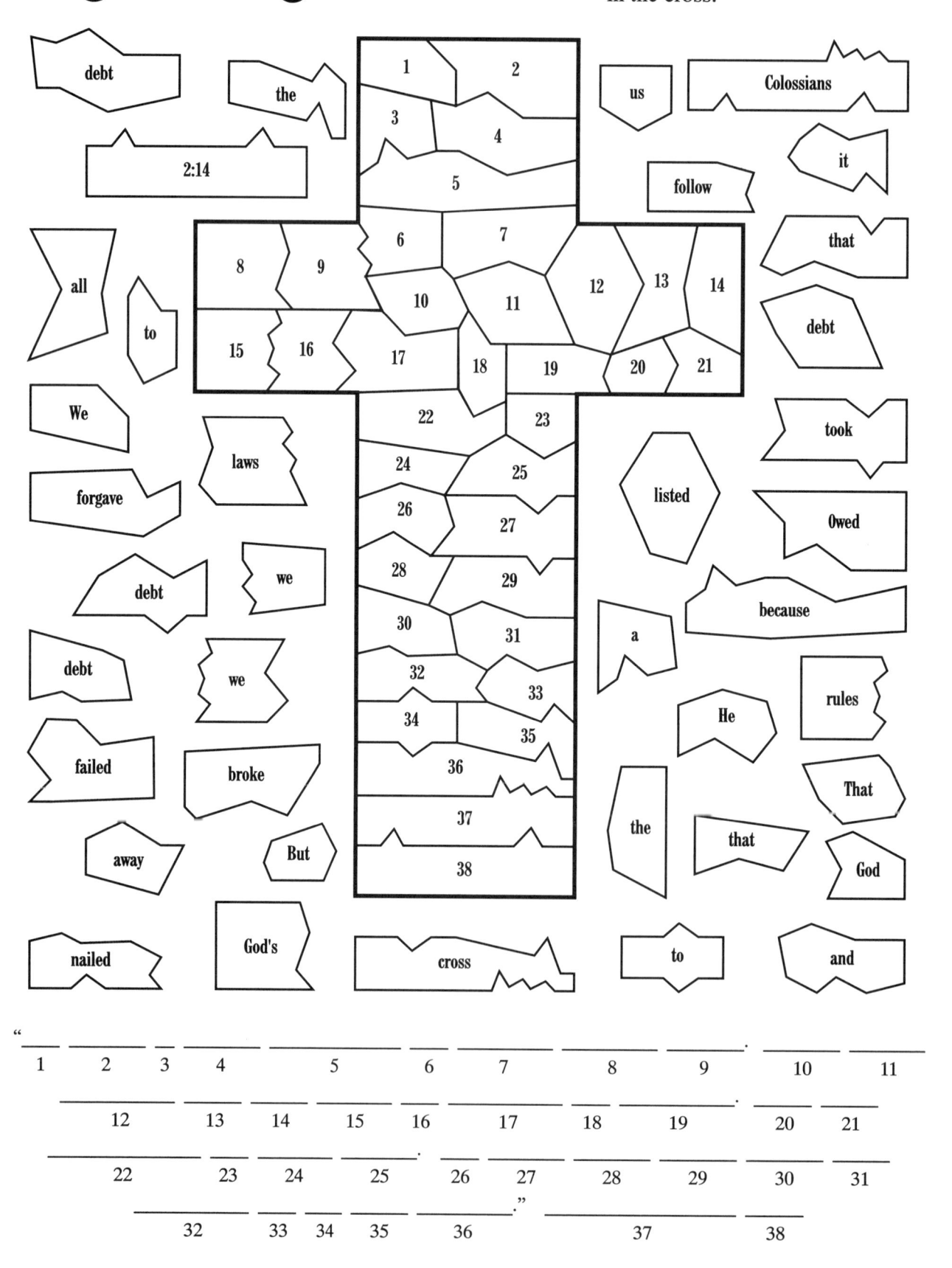

" ___ ___ ___ ___ ___ ___ ___ ___ ___ ___ ___ .
  1   2   3   4   5   6   7   8   9   10 11

___ ___ ___ ___ ___ ___ ___ ___ ___ ___ .
 12 13 14 15 16 17 18 19 20 21

___ ___ ___ ___ ___ ___ ___ ___ ___ ___
 22 23 24 25 26 27 28 29 30 31

___ ___ ___ ___ ___ ___ ___ ."
 32 33 34 35 36 37 38

7B © 1994 by The STANDARD PUBLISHING COMPANY. Permission is granted to photocopy this page for ministry purposes only—not for resale.

If we _____, then God forgives.	True or False?	Verse(s)
1. believe in Jesus	T F	
2. are truly sorry	T F	
3. confess sins to God in prayer	T F	
4. stop evil ways and obey God	T F	
5. never repeat the same sin twice	T F	
6. never sin again	T F	
7. forgive others	T F	
8. don't forgive ourselves	T F	

1 John 1:9   2 Chronicles 7:14   Acts 2:38
Psalm 32:5   Matthew 6:14, 15   Mark 11:25
Acts 10:43

What one-time event in Acts 2:38 leads to forgiveness? _____

Which of the above are part of repenting? Use a dictionary if you need to. _____

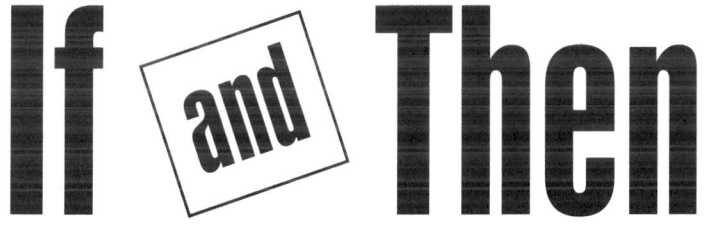

If and Then

Which of the phrases above correctly finish the sentence, "If we _____, then God forgives"? Prove which are true by reading the Bible verses listed. Write the Scripture references next to the phrases they match. The true phrases may have more than one reference. The false phrases have none.

© 1994 by The STANDARD PUBLISHING COMPANY. Permission is granted to photocopy this page for ministry purposes only—not for resale.

7C

Bible Story: Pray for Help to Do Right
Matthew 3:13-17

Unit 2: God Answers When We Pray
Session 8

Worship Focus: Worship God because He knows and judges us for what we do.

Obeying God

Transition Time
10-15 minutes

Send the children in small groups to the rest rooms and drinking fountain; then involve them in the following activity.

It's a Secret! Give each pupil a piece of drawing paper. Have pupils find a place in the room, distancing themselves from others. Each pupil will secretly draw a design using only straight lines, filling the page. No names are to be on the papers. Collect the designs and display them in the room.

Launching the Theme
10 minutes

Instruct the class to remain silent until you ask a question. Choose two pupils to be judges. The judges will distribute the "It's a Secret!" papers to the people they think drew them. **How many of you got your own papers?** (Allow responses.) **What was the judges' problem?** (Judges didn't know who drew the pictures.)

Our judges didn't see what you were drawing, but they judged who the papers' owners were anyway. We have a judge who sees and knows all, so His judgments are always right. Who is this judge? (God.) Read Jeremiah 23:24. **This verse tells us that God sees everything and is everywhere. He is our righteous judge who knows our hearts. Today we will worship God because He knows and judges us for what we do.**

Building the Theme
30 minutes

E easy   **I** independent   **A** advanced

1 Call to Worship **E**

Pupils will write examples of what God sees or hears using each letter of the alphabet. You will need Bibles, a roll of paper, and markers.

We will look at three verses that tell what God knows about us. Read Job 34:21; Proverbs 5:21; and Isaiah 37:28. After each verse, have pupils repeat the phrase that tells about God's knowledge. **Think of something God sees or hears us do, for each alphabet letter.** Write on the top edge of the paper, "God sees or hears me . . ." Ask for words that complete the title and begin with the letter A, such as "awake." Let volunteers write the words. Continue with the other alphabet letters, unrolling the paper as you go. **God knows everything we do.** Have pupils read Psalm 119:168, repeating it several times from memory.

For *Sharing in Worship*, pupils will read or pantomime some of their words and recite Psalm 119:168.

2 Drama A

Pupils will prepare skits to be performed after the Call to Worship. Provide Bibles, copies of Activity Page 8A, pencils, a tape player and blank cassette tape.

In the verses we will read, look for something God knows about us, besides what we look like or what we do. Read Psalm 139:1-6. **What else does God know?** (Our thoughts.)

Sometimes we do the right things, but don't think the right thoughts or have the right attitude. You will use the activity page to finish short skits to perform for the class. Work through the activity page with the group. Divide the parts and tape record the thoughts. Assign someone the task of running the tape player. Practice until the skits run smoothly.

3 Devotion A

Pupils will write a parable in the form of a children's book. You will need Bibles, copies of the top half of Activity Page 8B, large sheets of white construction paper, pencils, markers, and a stapler.

What is a parable? (A story that uses situations or objects people know to explain something they don't know.) **We will write a parable to explain two things about God found in Hebrews 4:13 and Ecclesiastes 12:14. What do these verses say about God?** (God knows and God judges.) **God allows us to choose whether or not we will obey Him. He knows everything we do and judges us for our actions. This is what our parable will explain, without even mentioning God. The activity page explains more about the parable. You will each have at least one page to write and illustrate. We will put the pages together to make a book.**

Distribute and read through the activity page with the group. Help pupils with the actual wording of each page, adding or combining pages as needed. Have pupils decide on a title, make the cover of the book, and staple it together.

Pupils will read their book during *Sharing in Worship,* along with Hebrews 4:13 and Ecclesiastes 12:14.

4 Music

Pupils will make a chart and prepare songs for worship. Provide Bibles, poster board, markers, and words to the song, "Trust and Obey." A volunteer will use the chart to introduce the songs.

Make three columns on the poster board, labeling them "Scripture," "Song," and "Sung for God or People?" **God knows what we do and is pleased when we obey Him. We will practice songs today about obeying and use them to complete this chart.** For the last column, pupils will decide whether each song is written to instruct people or as a praise to God.

Have pupils read James 1:22 for the song, "Trust and Obey." Read the song words and complete the chart.

For the second song, have the group read Psalm 119:9-11. Pupils will sing verses 9 and 10 to the tune of "Ten Little Indians." Ask pupils to name the song, adding it to the chart. The verses need to be written on a separate piece of poster board.

The last song uses the words of Psalm 19:14 sung to the tune of, "Twinkle, Twinkle, Little Star": "I hope my words and thoughts please you. Lord, you are . . . the one who saves me" *(ICB).* Have pupils choose a title and complete the chart. This verse also must be written on a separate piece of poster board.

5 Scripture I

Pupils in this group will make a poster of God's promises to those who obey. Provide Bibles, copies of the bottom half of Activity Page 8B, poster board, blue and red construction paper, scissors, tape or glue, pencils, and markers.

God knows and judges what we do. He promises special things to those who choose to obey Him. We are going to read some Bible promises from verses on this activity page. As you read through each verse, help pupils summarize the promises in one or two words. Each pupil will cut a star and write the summary and Scripture reference on it. Temporarily place, but do not attach, the stars to the poster board, leaving as much room in the center as possible. Have one pupil draw a person's outline in the center space with the title, "Promises for Those Who Obey." **Which stars do you find most encouraging?** (Allow responses.)

During *Sharing in Worship,* pupils will tape or glue stars onto the poster board as they read their summary words.

6 Prayer

Pupils will lead the class in writing prayer reminders and will conclude with a group prayer. Provide Bibles, paper, self-adhesive note pads, pencils or pens, and markers.

Jesus pleased God by obeying Him. We want to please God also, but sometimes it is hard to obey. Today we will pray for God's help. There are many ways to say, "God, help me obey." What other words could we use instead of "help"? (Write suggestions individually on paper, such as, *lead, show, teach, guide, strengthen, remind, assist,* and *direct.*) **Let's see what words these verses use.** Have pupils read Psalms 139:23, 24; 143:10 and identify words that could be synonyms for "help." (*Lead; teach.*) For a closing sentence prayer, divide the synonyms among the pupils. One person will begin with, "God, please," the others will each add their synonym, such as, "help me," "lead me," "show me," etc., ending with, "to obey Your Word."

Two of God's commandments are in Luke 10:27. Ask a student to read the verse. **Sometimes it is hard for us to be as loving as God wants. I am going to give each of you a piece of notepaper. First, write "God, help me obey. Help me . . . ," leaving room to finish the sentence. Think of a way you could be more loving toward others. Add it to the note. This will be your prayer reminder. You can put it in your Bible, notebook, or wherever you will see it.** Count out prayer reminders for the rest of the class, including teachers. The group will write, "God, help me obey. Help me . . . " on each one. They will instruct the rest of the class in finishing the reminders during worship.

Ask for several volunteers to end the worship time by offering sentence prayers praising God and thanking Him for His help in doing right.

Sharing in Worship
• • • • • • • • • • • • • • • • • • • •
20-25 minutes

If you did not have pupils do all the activities, plan to present them yourself or have another adult or two help you. Omit any activity that is to involved for you to do without help from the group.

Call to Worship
We are worshiping God because He knows and judges what we do. Group 1 made a list of things we do that God sees or hears. They will share a verse first, then read (or pantomime) some things from their list.

Drama
God knows everything about us, even what we think, why we do things, and how we feel about doing them. Group 2 will perform some skits. For each one you will hear a recording of one character's thoughts.

Devotion
Group 3 will read a parable and two verses explaining it. Listen carefully because I will ask you some questions.

Group 3 reads the parable and verses. **Think about the verses. What is this parable about?** (God knows what we do and judges us.) **If the fifth grader and the friend represent all people, who does the guard represent?** (God.) **What was the fifth grader's sin?** (Disobeying rules and lack of love for others.) **What was the judgment for the fifth grader?** (Can't skate.) **For the friend?** (Can skate again, free.)

God knows the good and bad we do and is pleased when we do right. God was pleased with what Jesus did. Jesus went to John to be baptized. He didn't do this because He had sinned. He did it in obedience to God. Right after His baptism, the Spirit of God took the form of a dove and landed on Him. God announced that Jesus was His son and that He loved Him and was pleased with Him.

When Jesus returns, God will judge us for what we do. Last week we talked about forgiveness. It is important to remember that God will forgive those who obey His Son. Still, everyone sins from time to time, and there are consequences for sin. **What was the consequence of the fifth grader's sin?** (Hurt others. He couldn't skate anymore. The guard didn't trust him.) Sometimes we hurt others when we sin. Sometimes we hurt ourselves. And we always hurt God. But God has promised to forgive us when we repent and try to obey Him.

Since God knows all that we do, think, and feel, and judges us for our actions, what should we do? (Obey Him.)

Music
Group 4 will lead songs about obeying. While you sing, pay close attention to the words.

Lord's Supper
God loves us and wants us to obey. He sent Jesus to die for us, taking our sins, so we can be forgiven and have the opportunity to live forever in Heaven. Use the quiet time now to think about Jesus, God's great gift.

Offering
We obey by giving our tithes and offerings to God.

Scripture
God promises special things to those who obey Him. Group 5 will share some of these with you. Pupils read their stars and tape or glue them onto the poster board.

Prayer
Group 6 began some prayer reminders for you. **They will tell you how to finish them.** After the class finishes, volunteers from Group 6 will pray the closing sentence prayers.

Closing Moments
10-15 minutes

Are You Obeying? Distribute copies of Activity Page 8C. Pupils should work individually on the page to help them apply today's worship focus.

God Knows our hearts and minds

Finish the skits below. Any of the verses from the bottom of the page can be read after each skit. The thoughts (in **bold** type) need to be taped and played back when the skits are performed.

DENISE: Hi. My name is Denise.
STEPHANIE: Hi, I'm Stephanie. Nice outfit. **Her clothes are the ugliest I've ever seen.**
BIBLE VERSE:

TEACHER: John, work problem six on the chalkboard.
JOHN: Sure. **She's so mean! Why does she always call on me?**
BIBLE VERSE:

MOTHER: Andy, your room looks awful! Get in there and pick it up!
ANDY: OK, Mom. No problem. **Gripe, gripe, gripe! I wish she'd get off my back!**
BIBLE VERSE:

KYLE: Can I ride your bike?
MARCUS: Yeah. I'm not riding it right now. **Why don't you buy your own bike and quit bothering me?**
BIBLE VERSE:

_____: Did you put money in the offering?
_____: _____
_____
_____
BIBLE VERSE:

_____: Would you please help me carry these boxes?
_____: _____
_____
_____
BIBLE VERSE:

Psalm 7:9
Psalm 44:20, 21
Proverbs 24:12
Proverbs 15:11
Acts 15:8
2 Chronicles 6:30
Luke 16:15

Make a Parable Book

Write a parable to explain two things about God found in Hebrews 4:13 and Ecclesiastes 12:14. Use the outline below. For each page, write the words and draw a picture to tell the story.

page 1: Introduce a character who loves to roller skate.
page 2: A friend agrees to go skating with the character.
page 3: All the way to the rink, the main character brags about being the best skater.
page 4: At the rink, the character shows off and ignores the friend.
page 5: The character pushes and knocks down several people.
page 6: A guard warns the character about the misbehavior.
page 7: The character ignores the guard and breaks even more skating rink rules.
page 8: The guard warns the character again.
page 9: The character calls the guard names and again ignores the warning.
page 10: The guard makes the character leave the rink.
page 11: Those still skating at the end, including the friend, get free skating passes.

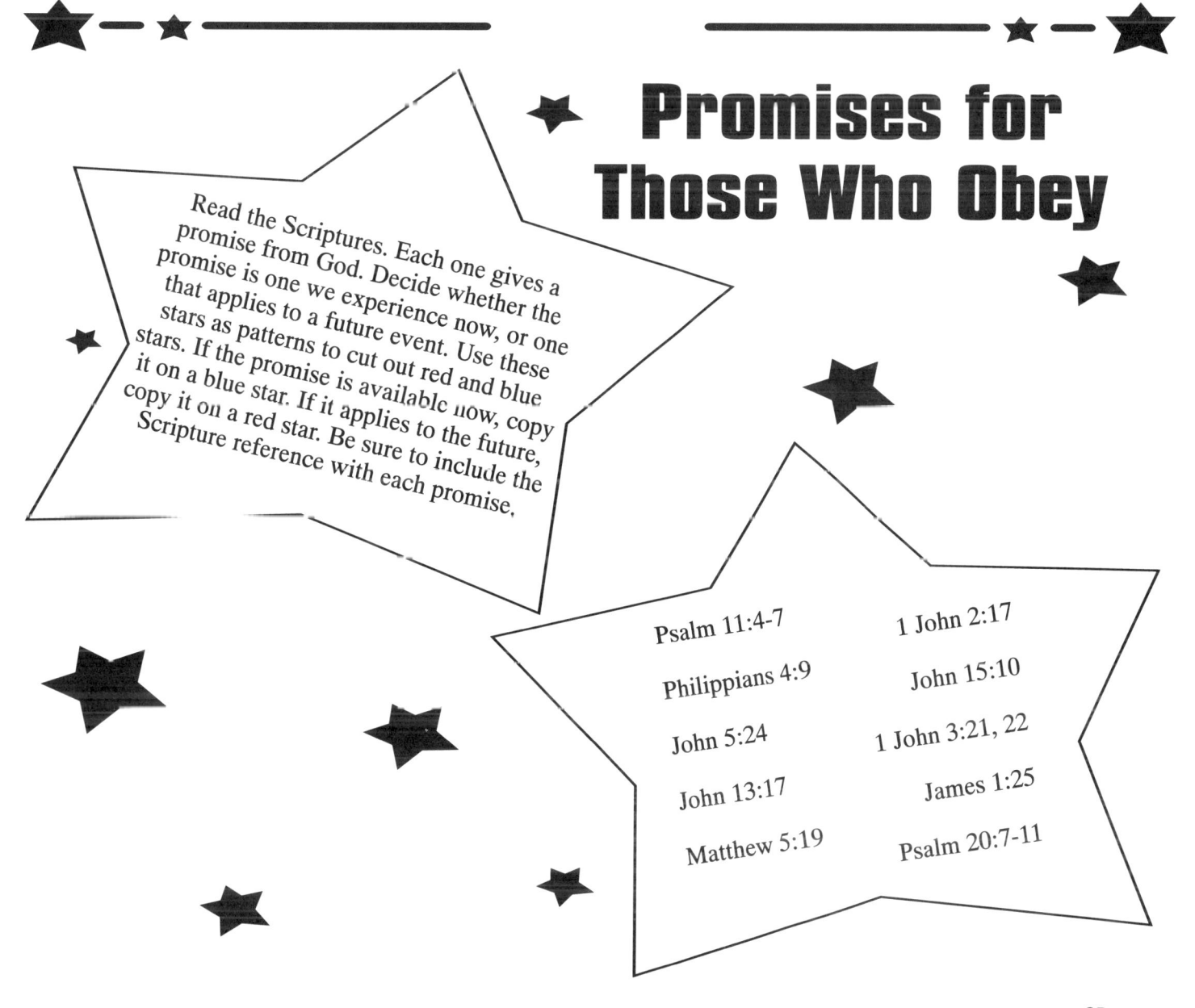

Promises for Those Who Obey

Read the Scriptures. Each one gives a promise from God. Decide whether the promise is one we experience now, or one that applies to a future event. Use these stars as patterns to cut out red and blue stars. If the promise is available now, copy it on a blue star. If it applies to the future, copy it on a red star. Be sure to include the Scripture reference with each promise.

Psalm 11:4-7
Philippians 4:9
John 5:24
John 13:17
Matthew 5:19

1 John 2:17
John 15:10
1 John 3:21, 22
James 1:25
Psalm 20:7-11

© 1994 by The STANDARD PUBLISHING COMPANY. Permission is granted to photocopy this page for ministry purposes only—not for resale.

Are You Obeying?

Do you make choices that please God? Rate each one of these to see areas in which you are obedient, and areas in which you need improvement. Make a mark on each line to show where you are.

I love my neighbor as myself.
Always |———————| Never

I share what I have with others.
Always |———————| Never

I am obedient to my parents.
Always |———————| Never

My language is appropriate and pure.
Always |———————| Never

I tell the truth.
Always |———————| Never

I obey persons in authority.
Always |———————| Never

I say and do what is right, even when others around me are not.
Always |———————| Never

I read and study the Bible every day.
Always |———————| Never

I express love for God.
Always |———————| Never

I watch only TV programs and videos God would like.
Always |———————| Never

I pray.
Always |———————| Never

I tell others about Jesus.
Always |———————| Never

Remember—God Sees Everything We Do

Draw a cartoon strip below about two people. In the first box, one person asks another a question. In the second box, the person asked answers with a lie. In the third box, the lie is discovered.

Bible Story: Pray for Help to Resist Temptation
Matthew 4:1-11

Unit 2: God Answers
When We Pray
Session 9

Worship Focus: Worship God because He gives strength and power to overcome temptation.

Overcoming Temptation

Transition Time
10-15 minutes

Send pupils in small groups to the rest rooms and drinking fountain. Set a tray of cookies in the room with a sign that says, "Do not touch."

Mouse Trap. Choose one child to sit in the center of the room, blindfolded. Mark off a four-foot square around him or her. Position half the class on each side of the blindfolded child, as far away as the room allows. **The square is a mousetrap. Each of you must walk quietly into the square and across the room. If the blindfolded child hears someone in the square, he says, "SNAP!" and that person is caught and must sit down.**

Launching the Theme
10 minutes

How is temptation like a mouse trap? (Allow responses.) **When a mouse gets caught, who's at fault, the cheese or the mouse?** (Mouse.) **The trapped mouse made a bad choice. When a trap's bait smells good to a mouse, the mouse gets closer and closer until it gets caught. For us, the bait is sin. We can choose to run from the trap or give in to temptation and get "caught" by sinning.**

We are tempted to do wrong things every day. **How many of you were tempted to cheat by not stepping in the mouse-trap square?** (Allow responses.) **How many of you saw the tray of cookies and wanted to take one?** (Allow responses.) **God knows when we are tempted and He can help us. Today we will worship God because He gives strength and power to overcome temptation.**

Distribute the cookies. Then summarize the activities for *Building the Theme* and allow each pupil to choose the group in which he or she would like to participate.

Building the Theme
30 minutes

E easy **I** independent **A** advanced

1 Call to Worship **E**
Pupils will design posters. Provide Bibles, poster board, letter stencils, magazines, children's coloring books, scissors, markers, crayons, pencils, and glue.

Who is tempted? (Everyone.) **God promises to be with those who trust and serve Him. He helps when they are tempted.** Read 1 Corinthians 10:13; 2 Peter 2:9; and Hebrews 13:5. Ask pupils to summarize each of these verses.

You will choose one of the verses we just read to put on a poster. Each poster needs a sentence explaining the verse and a picture to illustrate it. Pupils can work individually or in pairs and use any of the provided supplies to design their posters. The coloring book pages could be used to draw from or to color and glue to the poster board. During *Sharing in Worship*, pupils will show and read their posters.

2 Music

Pupils will prepare a medley for worship. Provide Bibles, poster board or an overhead projector with transparencies, and markers.

Do you know what a medley is? (A series of songs.) **We are going to sing a medley of three songs. The songs will remind us what God can do.** Read Ephesians 3:20. **Since God can do anything, we know He can help when we are tempted.**

Introduce the first song by singing the phrase, "Everyone is tempted, but just remember," to the tune of "Old MacDonald." Then sing the song, "My God Is So Great."

The second song is introduced with the sentence, "God gives power over temptation to those who follow Jesus," again using the tune of "Old MacDonald." Have pupils rewrite, "I've Got the Joy," to read, "God gives us pow'r, pow'r, pow'r, pow'r over temptation, over temptation, over temptation," adding an appropriate ending.

The third song is also sung to the tune of "Old MacDonald": "First we must remember to go to God for help, staying away from what is wrong and doing what is right. With a prayer prayer here and a prayer prayer there. Here a prayer, there a prayer. Everywhere a prayer prayer. Thank You, God, for all Your help. We love You." There is no introduction to this song.

Have pupils print song words on poster board or an overhead transparency. They can write extra stanzas as time allows.

Pupils from this group will lead their medley after the Call to Worship.

3 Lord's Supper

Pupils will complete an activity page to summarize two sets of verses. Provide Bibles, copies of Activity Page 9A, two large pieces of white construction paper, pencils, and markers.

What is your favorite sport? (Allow responses.) **Every sport has a winner and a loser. We will look at some verses that show how we can be winners.** Have pupils complete the activity page. (The answers and possible summaries in order are: Hebrews 2:18; Hebrews 4:15; Hebrews 12:3; Jesus was tempted but did not sin, so He can help us when we are tempted. He is our example. Acts 2:24; John 16:33; 1 John 4:4; God is greater than Satan and temptation. When God raised Jesus from the grave, Satan was defeated and Jesus was the winner. God can give us power and strength to be winners also.)

Divide the pupils into two groups. Assign either the top or bottom summary from the activity page for each group to write in the form of an outline of a cross. Pupils can then color the insides of the crosses and add "The Winner," as a title. Pupils will display and read their summaries before the Lord's Supper.

4 Devotion

Pupils will research sources of temptation and make a temptation tree. Provide Bibles, tan and blue construction paper, scissors, and thin markers.

Read James 1:13. Who does not tempt us? (God.) **We are going to find out from the Bible where temptation comes from. First, each of you will make a temptation tree by cutting tan construction paper into strips for a trunk and branches.**

Glue your strips onto the blue construction paper and add the title, "Temptation Tree." Have pupils make as many branches as possible.

You will read two Scriptures and write on the trunk what they say about temptation. First, read 1 Peter 5:8, 9. Write who these verses say is our enemy. (Satan.) **Now read James 1:14. What does this verse say tempts people?** (Evil desires.) **Satan uses our desires to tempt us. Write "desires" on the trunk. The Bible names desires that Satan uses. You will write these on the branches.** Have pupils read the following and write what Satan uses to tempt us: Luke 8:14 (worries, riches, and pleasures); Luke 21:34-36 (feasting, drinking, worldly things); and 1 Timothy 6:9, 10 (the love of money). On other branches, have pupils write specific temptations they face, such as disobeying parents.

For *Sharing in Worship*, pupils will read words from the trunk and branches as they display their trees.

5 Scripture A

Pupils will prepare skits about fighting temptation. Provide Bibles, copies of Activity Page 9B, pencils, a belt, vest (breastplate), shield, helmet, and sword.

The Bible tells about special armor to help us fight temptation. Have several pupils read Ephesians 6:10-18. **These actual clothes and objects don't help when we are tempted, but they represent attitudes and actions that help us obey God.** Discuss the following and what they represent: belt—gospel of truth; breastplate—right living; shoes—peace; shield—faith; helmet—salvation; and sword—Bible.

We are going to illustrate Ephesians 6:10-18 with skits. Help pupils complete the activity page and rehearse the skits.

If your group is small, let the pupils choose one or two situations they want to present. These will take place right after the Devotion.

6 Prayer I

Pupils will illustrate steps to a "prayer exercise." Provide Bibles, copies of Activity Page 9C, construction paper, pencils, and crayons or markers.

What are some things you are tempted to do? (Allow responses.) **Jesus gave us a strength-building exercise to help when we are tempted. The activity page will tell you what the exercise is.** (Allow time for students to complete the page.)

When Jesus taught about prayer, He told the disciples to ask God for help overcoming temptation. Read Matthew 6:9-13. **Since praying will give us strength over temptation, we will write steps to a "prayer exercise." The first step is a knee bend. What steps do you think would come next in preparing for prayer?** (Your prayer exercise could include: Knee bend and kneel, head bow, hand fold, eyes shut, and heart—talk to God.) Have pupils draw pictures portraying each portion of the exercise.

Pupils will display their pictures as they lead the exercise. Volunteers will give the closing prayer, asking God for strength.

Sharing in Worship
• • • • • • • • • • • • • • • • • • •
20-25 minutes

If you did not have pupils do all the activities, plan to present them yourself or have another adult or two help you. Omit any activity that is too involved for you to do without help from the group.

Call to Worship
We have come to worship our great God who gives us strength and power over temptation. Group 1 made posters to illustrate verses about the help God gives. Group 1 shows and reads their posters.

Music
Group 2 will lead a medley of three

songs about temptation. Let's sing with them.

Lord's Supper
This group will read summaries about Jesus' great victory over Satan. Group 3 shows their crosses and reads the summaries. **Jesus conquered Satan forever when He arose from the grave. God helps us be winners also. During our silent time now, thank God for His victorious Son, Jesus.**

Offering
God uses what we give for His work here on earth. He wants us to give joyfully and prayerfully. Let's give our offerings to Him now.

Devotion
Have available two pairs of sunglasses, Vaseline®, two sheets of drawing paper with an object to trace, and two pens or markers. **We need to recognize temptation so we can ask God to give us strength and power to overcome it. Group 4 will read some sources of temptation from their temptation trees.** Group 4 shows their trees and reads the words.

Jesus faced temptations also. After Jesus was baptized, God's Spirit led Him into the desert to pray and prepare for His ministry. Jesus did not eat for forty days, so Satan tempted Him with food. Jesus resisted the temptation by quoting Scripture. Then Satan tempted Him twice more. He tempted Jesus to show off and to desire money and power. Again, Jesus resisted by quoting from the Bible. Were the temptations Jesus faced on Group 4's temptation trees? (Yes. Desire for food; worldly attitude to show off, against God's will; desire for riches.) **We also can overcome temptation with God's Word.**

Give two volunteers sunglasses and paper with an object to trace. One pair of glasses must be thickly smeared with Vaseline®. The volunteers will trace the object while wearing the glasses. Show the class the finished papers. **What kept ____ from following the lines neatly?** (Couldn't see.) **When we don't keep our eyes and thoughts on Jesus and on obeying God, we can be tempted to go the wrong way also. We need to know what is right so we can stay away from what's wrong. How can we know the right things God wants us to do?** (Read Bible, pray, go to church and Sunday school, listen to parents and other Christian teachers.)

Scripture
God's Word, the Bible, can help us when we are tempted. The Bible tells about special armor that we can use to overcome temptation. Group 5 will role play some temptations and the right attitudes and actions to overcome them.

Prayer
Now that you've been sitting awhile, it is time for a "prayer exercise." Group 6 will show you how to do the exercise. After the exercise, volunteers will pray.

Closing Moments
10-15 minutes

Puzzled Messages. Beforehand, write the Worship Focus on construction paper, along with specifics from this session, such as, "God helps us stand up to temptation. He never leaves us. He gave Jesus as an example. He gives comfort and help in the Bible. He answers our prayers." Cut the sheet of messages into puzzle pieces and place in an envelope. Prepare puzzles and envelopes for each group of two or three pupils to assemble and read. To make the task more difficult, replace one puzzle piece from each envelope with a piece from a different puzzle. The pupils will need to visit other groups to find their missing pieces.

SUPER VICTORY

To find the correct victory Scriptures below, write the name or numeral in each pile that touches exactly three other names or numerals. Read the six verses and write a summary for each group.

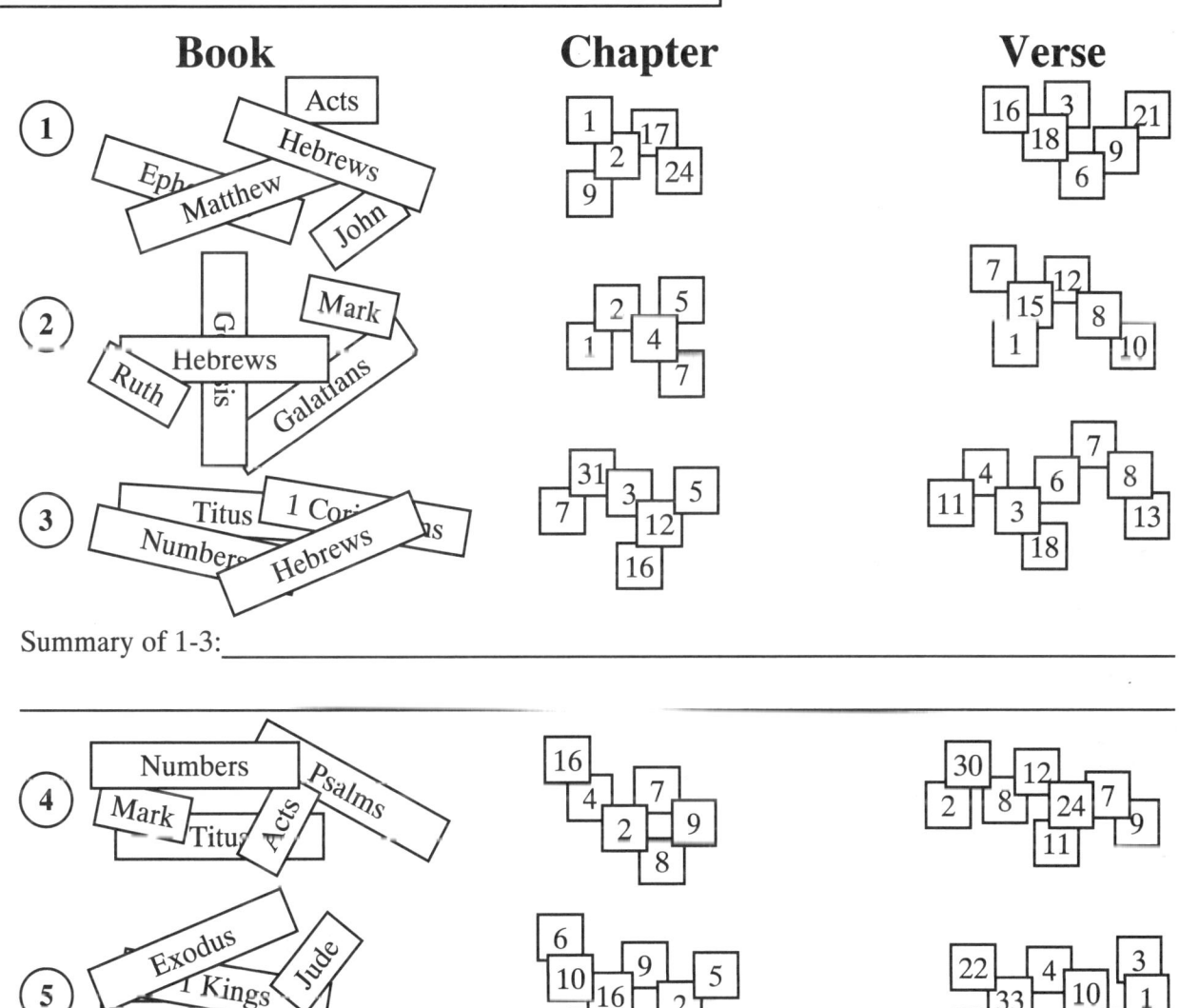

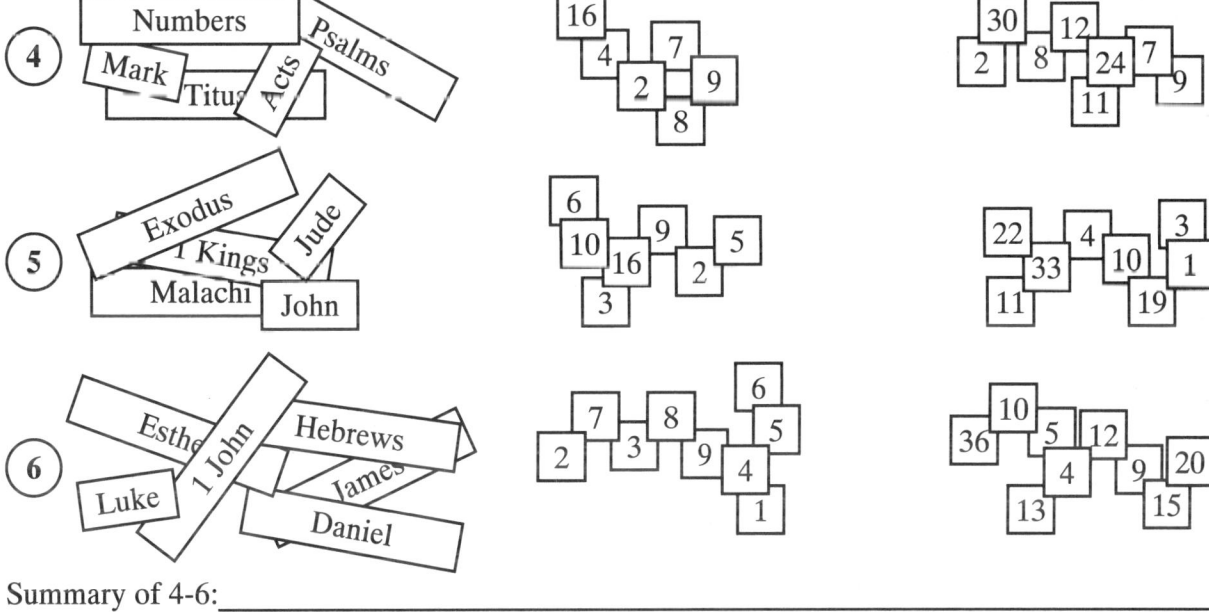

Book Chapter Verse

1) Acts, Hebrews, Eph…, Matthew, John

Chapter: 1, 17, 2, 24, 9

Verse: 16, 3, 18, 21, 9, 6

2) G…, Mark, Hebrews, Ruth, Galatians

Chapter: 2, 5, 1, 4, 7

Verse: 7, 12, 15, 8, 1, 10

3) Titus, 1 Cor…, Numbers, Hebrews

Chapter: 31, 3, 5, 7, 12, 16

Verse: 7, 4, 6, 8, 11, 3, 13, 18

Summary of 1-3: _____

---

4) Numbers, Psalms, Mark, Titus, Acts

Chapter: 16, 4, 7, 2, 9, 8

Verse: 30, 12, 2, 8, 24, 7, 11, 9

5) Exodus, Jude, 1 Kings, Malachi, John

Chapter: 6, 10, 9, 5, 16, 2, 3

Verse: 22, 4, 3, 33, 10, 1, 11, 19

6) Esther, 1 John, Hebrews, James, Luke, Daniel

Chapter: 6, 7, 8, 5, 2, 3, 9, 4, 1

Verse: 10, 36, 5, 12, 4, 9, 20, 13, 15

Summary of 4-6: _____

© 1994 by The STANDARD PUBLISHING COMPANY. Permission is granted to photocopy this page for ministry purposes only—not for resale. **9A**

PROTECTED BY ARMOR

The armor of God helps us to resist temptation. Read Ephesians 6:14-17 and fill in the chart. Make up examples of the different temptations to perform as skits. One has been done for you.

Choose performers and write their names on the chart, and decide who will read the verse from Ephesians. The skits should demonstrate how to resist temptation using the armor of God.

Verse	Piece of Clothing or Armor	Temptation	Example	Performers	Reader
14a		to lie	Jason accidently broke his mom's lamp. He is tempted to pretend he doesn't know what happened, but he decides to tell the truth.		
14b		to make fun of others			
15		to join an argument or gossip			
16		to believe God doesn't care about you			
17a		to get discouraged			
17b		not to forgive			

9B © 1994 by The STANDARD PUBLISHING COMPANY. Permission is granted to photocopy this page for ministry purposes only—not for resale.

Exercise Time

Begin with **A**, and cross off each letter of the alphabet. Every time you come to a letter that is missing, write it in the box. You will go through the alphabet 3 times to find a total of 15 missing letters. Unscramble the missing letters to discover an exercise that will help you overcome temptation. Read Matthew 26:41 for a clue.

J D P D Z L B
W Q I W Z J Q V H U
S Z
U X H P V X W A
O M L
C N Y A T O
E K K G
M G E M B V N
F U K I B I Q Y Z
S J C X F L D C

Missing Letters

Unscramble letters here:

_ _ _ _

_ _ _

_ _ _ _ _ _ _

© 1994 by The STANDARD PUBLISHING COMPANY. Permission is granted to photocopy this page for ministry purposes only—not for resale.

Bible Story: Jesus Chooses Special Disciples
Matthew 10:2-4; John 1:35-44

Unit 3: Jesus Teaches About Happiness
Session 10

Worship Focus: Worship God because He is worthy to be followed.

Worthy to Be Followed

Transition Time

10-15 minutes

Send the children in small groups to the rest rooms and drinking fountain. Welcome newcomers and involve everyone in the following activity.

Whom to Follow? Before class, gather several sports and celebrity magazines and newspapers, scissors, paper, and pencils.

As pupils arrive, have them look through the magazines and newspapers and ask each pupil to decide which one person he or she would be most likely to follow. Instruct pupils to cut out the pictures from the magazines or newspapers. Then have each pupil make a list of reasons why he or she would follow the person.

If you have a large group, cut out several pictures of popular people and display them on the wall for the pupils to choose from.

Whom did you choose to follow? (Allow each pupil to respond.) **Why would you want to follow this person?** (Allow pupils to state their reasons as you make a list on the chalkboard. For example: strong personality; good in front of people; great athlete; a good public speaker; has determination; follows through on promises made, and so on.)

Launching the Theme

10 minutes

Ask an adult in your church to dress as a prospector for gold and perform the monologue from Activity Page 10A. **Option:** Have pupils read the page or have it read aloud in class; then ask questions or lead a discussion about the story.

People went west to look for gold because they believed the promise that they could get rich quick. Many people promise us great things if we do what they say. But people cannot guarantee their promises. People are often wrong. Only God has the power and knowledge always to do what He says. Only God is never wrong. Thus, God is the only one who is worthy to be followed.

Briefly explain the choices of preparation for worship. Allow the children to choose their groups.

Building the Theme

30 minutes

E easy   **I** independent   **A** advanced

1 Call to Worship

Pupils will discover the meaning of "worthy," and make a mural about God's worthiness. You will need to supply one large piece of white glossy butcher paper, secured to the wall; a dictionary and Bible dictionary; several colors of pudding; and damp paper towels. Make sure you cover the floor surface with plastic or newspapers and have pupils use craft smocks.

Before the activity begins, make sure the pupils have washed their hands. The pupils will learn the definition of "worthy" and construct a finger painting mural to display during *Sharing in Worship*. The picture can illustrate the definition of "worthy" or it can express praise to God for being worthy. Have pupils place their finger(s) into the desired color of pudding and using the pudding, draw directly onto the paper. Instruct them that they may want to mix the different colors of pudding in as they paint.

What is the meaning of "worthy"? (A person of outstanding worth or importance; having worth, value, or merit; excellence resulting from superior moral, cultural, or spiritual qualities.) **Do you know of anyone who is worthy?** (Allow responses. God is worthy. God is head over all. He is the ruler of all things. He gives strength to everything.) **Do you think God is worthy to be followed?** (Allow response.)

Have one or more pupils prepare to read the definition aloud during *Sharing in Worship*. Others may hold up the group's mural as the definition is being read.

2 Music

Pupils will write and prepare to sing a special song. They will need a songbook with the song, "Thou Art Worthy," Bibles, paper, and pencils. A taped accompaniment will be helpful also.

Have pupils sing the song until they are familiar with it. Then have them read these Scriptures: Revelation 4:11; 5:9; 15:4. Instruct the pupils to write new words telling why God is worthy to be followed.

Singing is one way we can praise God because He is worthy to be followed. What can you see in these Scriptures that we can use in our new song? (Allow responses.) **We are going to sing this song in our worship time, then teach it to the rest of the group.**

Practice the song with the new words. This song will be performed as special music during *Sharing in Worship*.

3 Scripture

Pupils will create freeze frames about following Jesus. This activity will require Bibles, paper, and pencils.

Begin the activity by having the pupils read the following Scriptures: Matthew 16:24; 19:21; and Mark 10:28. **Name the things Jesus said we must be willing to do or give up for Him.** (Deny yourself and take up your cross and follow me; sell your possessions and give to the poor; leave everything.) Then instruct pupils to create freeze frames (still frames) for each item needed to be given up in order to follow Jesus. Assign parts for each scene and practice the scenes freeze style. In other words, no moving, no blinking, no nothing! They are frozen!

During *Sharing in Worship*, the pupils will present their freeze frames for the rest of the class.

4 Devotion A

Pupils will prepare scenes showing ways Bible people benefited from following God. Pupils will need copies of Activity Page 10B, an instant camera, a photo album with plenty of blank pages for the photos to be taken the next four weeks, Bible-times clothes and props, Bibles, and markers.

Help pupils prepare scenes portraying the way Bible people benefited from following God. Instruct the pupils to leave the first page of the album blank. Title the next three pages: (1) Name a time you chose to follow God. (2) Tell why you followed God. (3) Describe what happened when you followed God.

During the session, pupils will do the following: (1) Survey the Scriptures and answer the questions found on the three album pages. (2) From their answers, decide which scenes to portray. (3) Choose characters and props, pose the scenes, and take the photographs. (4) Mount and label pictures.

During *Sharing in Worship,* pupils will share the information from the photo album.

5 Praise Offering

Pupils will prepare a mobile showing things to give back in order to follow God. Provide a wire hanger, paper, catalogs and magazines, scissors, yarn or string of various lengths, and Bibles. If pupils will be working independently, tape record or write brief instructions to guide them.

Instruct the pupils in preparing the mobile. **I want you to list specific things that belong to you that you can give back to God.** Then have each pupil make a mobile piece, using a catalog or magazine picture, to illustrate one thing on the list.

During *Sharing in Worship,* each pupil will tie a mobile piece to the hanger and say, "God is worthy to have (the thing illustrated)."

6 Prayer

Pupils will prepare to lead prayer groups. Pupils will need copies of Activity Page 10C and Bibles.

Read the Scriptures and help pupils choose one thing in each verse for which to thank God. Revelation 4:11 (power in creation); Revelation 5:9 (salvation); Revelation 15:3b, 4 (His character, righteous, true, just); Revelation 11:15b, 17 (His Son).

These Scriptures state reasons God is worthy to be followed. Can you think of any other reasons God is worthy to be followed? (Allow pupils to add additional reasons.)

Set up four prayer stations in the room with at least two pupils at each station. During *Sharing in Worship,* worshipers will choose a station. A leader at each station will read one of the Scriptures from the activity page and suggest a reason to thank God. The participants will then pray silently. Ask worshipers to move to other stations at your signal.

Sharing in Worship
20-25 minutes

If you did not have the pupils do all the activities, plan to present them yourself, or have another adult or two help you. Omit any activity that is too involved for you to do without help from the group.

Call to Worship
Group 1 has made a mural, explaining the word *worthy*. Have one pupil give the definition. Then have the other pupils from the group take turns telling about their mural.

Music
Have Group 2 lead the rest of the group in singing "Thou Art Worthy!" Then have them sing their new stanzas as special music.

Scripture
Group 3 has created freeze frames about the things God has told us we must give up in order to follow Him. Have the group present their freeze frames using Matthew 16:24; Matthew 19:21; and Mark 10:28.

Lord's Supper
We have been worshiping God because He is worthy to be followed. His Son, Jesus, is the only One who was willing and able to die for the wrong things we

do. He is the only One with the power to come back from the dead. These are important reasons Jesus is also worthy to be followed. Let's remember Jesus' death for our sins now.

Devotion

When Jesus began His earthly ministry, many people gathered around to hear Him. Two men began to follow Jesus at once. Some followed Jesus because they wanted to know more about Jesus. Andrew felt that Jesus was the promised Messiah, so he wanted his brother to know Him too. Jesus did not wait for Andrew to introduce his brother. Jesus already knew who Simon was and gave him a new name, Peter. Along the way, several other men responded to Jesus by joining this special group.

Many people wanted to follow Jesus no matter what their lives were like before meeting Jesus. They gave up their families, their homes, their friends to follow Jesus. Why would they do this? Because they believed that Jesus was from God and was worthy to be followed.

Do you want to follow God? (Allow response.) Do you understand that God is worthy to be followed? Will you follow Him today? What will you give up to follow God? Your friends? Your family? God doesn't ask you to leave home and family right now to follow Him. He does expect You to put Him first in your life, ahead of TV, sports, and anything else that is important to you. God is worthy to be followed. The disciples thought so many years ago, and we do today.

Group 4 has prepared scenes portraying the ways Bible people benefited from following God. Have the members of Group 4 present the information from their photo album.

Offering

One way we can follow God is by giving back part of what He has given to us. While the offering is being taken, have members of Group 5 tie their mobile pieces to the hanger one at a time and say, "God is worthy to have (the thing illustrated)."

Prayer

Have one or two members from this group at each prayer station. **Choose one of the prayer stations and quietly move to that station.** (Make sure pupils are fairly evenly divided among the stations.) The leaders at each station will read one of the Scriptures from the activity page and suggest a reason to thank God. The participants will then pray silently. Ask worshipers to move to other stations at your signal.

Closing Moments

10-15 minutes

Blind Walk. Explain to pupils that this game will be a lesson in trusting and following. Divide the class evenly into teams. Line the teams up at one end of the classroom. Teams will work in pairs. One member of each pair is blindfolded and will be led by his or her partner around obstacles (the same number for each team). When the pair arrives at the designated point at the other end of the room, the blindfold is removed. The pairs run back to their teams, pass the blindfolds to the next pairs, and sit at the ends of their lines. If a team member steps on or touches an obstacle, he must be led back to the beginning and walk the path again. The first team with all members seated wins.

Jeb, the Gold Prospector

Hello there! My name is Jeb, and I'm a San Francisco 49'er. Now hold on. Don't get too excited. I don't play any football, if that's what you're thinkin'. I'm a San Francisco 49'er from back in eighteen hundred and forty-nine—over one hundred years ago.

Now, I lived in Missouri you see. I was a farmer. I had a family and some kids. An' one day this fella came to town and was goin' on and on about gold in Californee. Tons of gold he said . . . worth more money than you could spend in a lifetime. Now, my farming wasn't goin' too well so I figured it would be worth it for me to run on down to Californee and gather up some of that gold. Thought I'd come right on back to Missouri and we'd have more money than any of these folks around here had ever seen.

So, I set off with that man. Left my wife, my kids, my home, and about everything I had worked for in the last thirty years. Hey, but it was worth it because I was goin' to be a rich man!

Uh, the trip to Californee was long. Took about three months. We crossed more mountains and rivers than I could count. But finally we were there. San Francisco, the gold mining town. Well, I got myself some gold mining equipment and an old metal pan with holes punched in the bottom and I started panning gold. I'd dip that pan in the bottom of a river until it was full of dirt and rocks and water. And then I'd lift it out and let the water and loose dirt run out the holes in the bottom. Uh, hopefully, there would be some big gold nuggets left in the bottom of the pan. I panned for gold all that day. And then the next day. And the next. No gold. Not one bit! Well, I'd be happy with a little chunk of gold by that time. But I couldn't find anything but rocks and dirt.

I stayed in San Francisco for two years looking for my gold. Well, I did find some. Enough to feed myself and for clothes to wear. But nothing more. Finally I gave it up and went home with no gold. I was ruined! My farmland had been sold to provide for my family while I was gone. Now I had nothing! I left EVERYTHING to follow that man who promised me gold and he had been wrong!

SAY CHEESE!

Read these Scriptures and answer the questions. Then, using Bible-times clothes and props, prepare scenes portraying how Bible people benefitted from following God. Pose the scenes and take instant photographs. Label the photos and mount them in an album.

Acts 16:11-34   Acts 8:26-40   Matthew 4:18, 19
                                             Matthew 16:13-18
                                             Acts 2:37-41

1. Describe a time the person chose to follow God.

2. Tell why the person chose to follow God.

3. What happened as a result of his obedience?

© 1994 by The STANDARD PUBLISHING COMPANY. Permission is granted to photocopy this page for ministry purposes only—not for resale.

God Is Worthy

Read the Scriptures and list reasons God is worthy of our praise and our obedience.

Revelation 4:1

Revelation 5:9

Revelation 15:3b, 4

Revelation 11:15b, 17

Bible Story: Jesus' Sermon on the Mount
Matthew 5:1-12

Unit 3: Jesus Teaches About Happiness
Session 11

Worship Focus: Worship God because He gives us lasting joy.

I've Got the Joy Down in My Heart

Transition Time
10-15 minutes

After the pupils have had time to go to the rest rooms and drinking fountain, involve them in the following activity.

"**AD-itudes.**" Begin the activity by having pupils stand facing you as you call out one of the following words: bad, sad, glad, mad, and so on. Pupils must make a face that matches the word called. Start calling the words out slowly and speed up. If a pupil makes the wrong face, he or she is out.

Optional: Before this activity begins, you may want to display a long mirror or provide several hand mirrors for pupils to use during the activity. Kids love looking at themselves and each other in mirrors.

Launching the Theme
10 minutes

Before this activity begins, display a batch of cookies, several Nintendo® games, and a new item of clothing on a table.

Hey, I brought you some cookies today. (Share the cookies with the pupils as you continue the discussion.) **How did you feel when you found out I brought cookies to class and wanted to share them with you?** (Allow for responses.) **How would you feel if I told you that you had won ten Nintendo® games?** (Hold up games for pupils to see.) **Or, a new item of clothing?** (Hold up item of clothing and allow pupils to respond to each question.) **There are many things that make us happy. What other things make you happy?** (Pupils respond.)

All these things make us feel happy for a little while, but after we eat chocolate chip cookies, we soon feel hungry again. We get tired of playing Nintendo® games. Our new clothes get old or we outgrow them. Only God gives us happiness that lasts. True happiness is often called joy. Today we will worship God because He gives us lasting joy.

Briefly explain the choices of preparation for worship. Allow the children to choose the groups in which they would like to participate.

Building the Theme
30 minutes

E easy   **I** independent   **A** advanced

1 Call to Worship **E**
Pupils will make a montage of "rainbow" writing using words that describe ways

God gives us joy. For this activity you will need to provide Bibles, white construction paper, colored chalk, hair spray, water, and paper towels.

Ask pupils to make a list of ways God gives us joy, based on the following Scriptures: Psalm 16:11 (His presence); Psalm 51:12 (His salvation); Psalm 67:4 (He rules and guides); Romans 14:17 (Holy Spirit); Philippians 1:3, 4 (other Christians); 1 Peter 1:8, 9 (salvation of our souls). **What sources of Christian joy are listed in the Scripture?** (Allow pupils to respond. List these on the chalkboard.) **Select a source of Christian joy from the list to write, using chalk, and outline in joyful colors.** (As each color is added, the word wil become larger.) Spray the completed montage with hair spray.

During *Sharing in Worship*, ask each pupil to tell about a way God gives us joy, using his or her drawing.

2 Music

Pupils will research "joy" Scriptures and learn to sing a song. For this activity, pupils will need words and music to "I've Got the Joy, Joy, Joy, Joy"; Bibles; paper; and pencils. A tape recording of the song will be helpful.

Play the song several times for the pupils so they can become familiar with the tune and words of the song. **Let's read the following Scriptures concerning the joy that God gives us.** Psalm 16:11 (Fill me with Your joy); Psalm 100:1 (Shout joy to God); Luke 6:23 (Rejoice for today and leap with joy); Philippians 4:4 (Rejoice in the Lord); Romans 15:13 (Be filled with joy and peace). **Can someone put each Scripture into a simple sentence or statement?** (Allow pupils to paraphrase each Scripture.) Write the statements on the chalkboard and ask each pupil to choose one statement to say. Sing the song through again. A pupil will say one statement during the song at the point when the pupils usually shout, "Where?"

During *Sharing in Worship*, the group will sing their song, along with the statements of joy.

3 Scripture

For this activity you will need copies of Activity Page 11A, paper cups, Styrofoam pieces (about 1" to 1 ½" thick), green chenille wires, ribbon or yarn, tape, glue, and scissors. Pupils will create "Hearts of Joy" flower arrangements to be given to others on Valentine's Day.

Have pupils cut out the hearts from the activity page. **God gives us joy in many ways. Can you tell me one way God gives you joy?** (Allow pupils to respond.) **It is important for us to let other people know that God can give them joy also.** Give each pupil a piece of Styrofoam to glue inside the bottom of a paper cup. Then instruct pupils to cut six chenille wires into various lengths; insert the wires into the Styrofoam, and tape each of the six hearts to a chenille wire. Tie pieces of ribbon or yarn around the tops of the paper cups.

During *Sharing in Worship*, the pupils will display their "Hearts of Joy" flower arrangements. Encourage the pupils to give their arrangements to people they love.

4 Devotion A

Pupils will prepare modern-day scenes that portray people demonstrating some of the Beatitudes. Pupils will need the photo album used last week, copies of Activity Page 11B, an instant camera, Bibles, and markers.

Have pupils read the Beatitudes in Matthew 5:3-12 and then complete the activity page. Instruct the pupils to label several pages in the album, "Jesus Gives Us Joy." Ask pupils to pose modern-day situations, each of which illustrates one of the Beatitudes.

During *Sharing in Worship*, the pupils will show and explain the pictures in the photo album.

5 Personal Praise

Each pupil will make a "Joy" flag and write a statement of praise. Pupils will need fabric scraps or old bed sheets (solid color or white), dowel rods, scissors, hot glue gun (for adults only), glue sticks, and black markers.

Since God has given us joy, we need to keep it in our hearts. What else should we do with the joy God has given us? (Let the whole world know.) **We will create "Joy" flags to remind us and to tell others of that great joy God has given us. One way we can praise God is to share His joy with others.**

Help pupils design and cut flags out of the fabric or sheets to fit the dowel rods (cut squares, triangles, rectangles, etc.). Then have them write the word *JOY* in bold letters on the flags. An adult should glue the flags onto the dowel rods.

After the flags are completed, each pupil will write a statement of praise to God for a way He gives lasting joy. (For example, "I praise God for the joy of living in a Christian home." Or, "I praise God that He gives me joy in the world He has created."

During *Sharing in Worship*, the group will wave their "Joy" flags while Group 2 leads their song. After the Offering, Group 5 will hold up their flags and take turns praising God for joys.

6 Prayer

Each pupil will draw a cartoon strip to thank God for specific joys He has given. Pupils will need Bibles, paper, and pencils. If pupils will be working independently, either tape record or write brief instructions for them to follow.

Have the pupils look up and read Philippians 4:4. **Philippians 4:4 tells us to rejoice in the Lord always. Can you think of a specific time this past week when God helped you to be joyous?** (Allow responses. For example: I didn't feel like going to church because I stayed up late the night before. When I got to church, I listened to the teacher. I felt happy knowing I had done the right thing by going to church even if I didn't feel like it.) Pupils are to draw cartoon strips, using speech balloons, thanking God for giving joy at specific times during the past week.

At the end of *Sharing in Worship*, each of you will show and read your cartoon strip. Ask for several volunteers to pray sentence prayers to close.

Sharing in Worship
20-25 minutes

If you did not have pupils do all the activities, plan to present them yourself or have another adult or two help you. Omit any activity that is too involved for you to do without help from the group.

Call to Worship
Group 1 has made a montage of "rainbow" writings that describe ways God gives us joy. Have group members display and explain their montage.

Music
Many songs tell about the joy of the Lord. Group 2 will sing one of them at this time. Have Group 2 sing the song with the added statements during the song. Then sing the song again, having the rest of the class join in singing, while Group 5 waves their "Joy" flags.

Scripture
Group 3 has also created "Hearts of Joy" flower arrangements that describe ways God gives us joy. Have one member read the appropriate Scriptures from the joy hearts while their "Hearts of Joy" flower arrangements are being displayed.

Devotion
This week we are celebrating Valentine's Day. This is a day designed

to share feelings of love with others. You may have discovered, however, that this is not a very good time of year for classmates who are not well liked. But because Jesus stood on a hillside many years ago and talked about how to be happy, we are able to show love on Valentine's Day, and on other days of the year, to those we love, as well as to those we may not like. When we realize we are not perfect, we are more able to be kind and show love to others, who are not perfect, either.

God has given us a special Valentine's Day present. What is it? (His joy.) **His joy is for everyone. And He gives us joy in more ways than we can count!**

Members of Group 4 have prepared modern-day scenes that illustrate some of the Beatitudes. Have members of Group 4 share their information from the photo album.

Lord's Supper

First Peter 1:8 and 9 tells us that knowing Jesus has saved us gives us so much joy we cannot even explain it. Let's remember and thank God for the joy we have because Jesus took the punishment for our sins.

Offering

One way we can praise God for the lasting joy He gives is by giving joyfully back to Him. Let's read 2 Corinthians 9:7. Do so at this time.

Personal Praise

Group 5 has made special flags to help remind us to remain joyful and tell others about our joy. Have members read or say their praise statements as they display their flags.

Prayer

Group 6 has designed some cartoon strips that thank God for giving joys during this past week. Allow the group to show their pictures. Then form a circle and have volunteers pray sentence prayers.

Closing Moments

10-15 minutes

The Heart-of-It-All Puzzle. For this activity you will need copies of Activity Page 11C, Bibles, scissors, and glue. Complete instructions for this activity are given on the activity page so it can be done without adult guidance.

After pupils have completed the activity, have them quote the verse together as a class. **When we have been filled with God's joy, what are we going to receive?** (The salvation of our souls.)

HEARTS OF JOY

Read the Scripture on each heart and write a short description of a way God gives us joy. Then cut out the hearts or use them as patterns to cut hearts out of construction paper and write on them. Attach the hearts to chenille wires and arrange them in a styrofoam cup as shown.

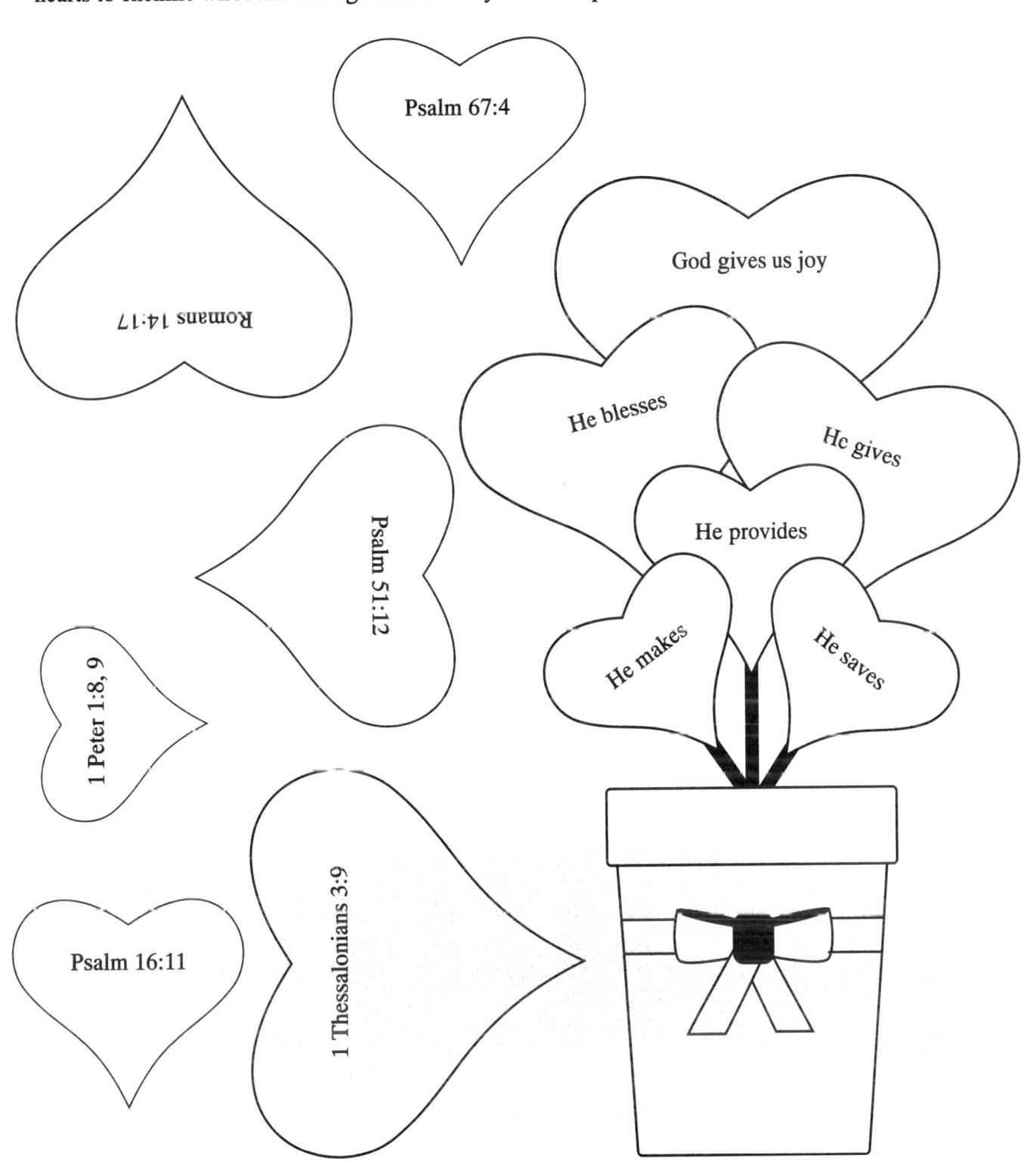

- Psalm 67:4
- Romans 14:17
- Psalm 51:12
- 1 Peter 1:8, 9
- 1 Thessalonians 3:9
- Psalm 16:11

God gives us joy
- He blesses
- He gives
- He provides
- He makes
- He saves

© 1994 by The STANDARD PUBLISHING COMPANY. Permission is granted to photocopy this page for ministry purposes only—not for resale.   11A

Joy for All Occasions

Match the Scripture to the real-life situation in which a person demonstrates one of the Beatitudes.

- Jesse wants to do right as much as he wants to eat when he's hungry or drink when he is thirsty. He uses every opportunity to learn more about what God wants him to do.

- Shadi realizes if he fills his mind with evil things, his actions will be affected. He knows to fill his mind with the best kinds of thoughts and leave no room to mix in impure thoughts.

- Peter knows he needs the Lord in his life. He asks God to help him because Peter knows he can't succeed alone.

- Emi backed out of a fight. She learned it does not mean she has a lack of courage. She was brave enough to stop the fight by being a peacemaker.

Matthew 5:3   Matthew 5:7
Matthew 5:4   Matthew 5:8
Matthew 5:5   Matthew 5:9
Matthew 5:6   Matthew 5:10

- Drew is sometimes ridiculed because of his beliefs. He stands up for what is right, no matter what other people do or say.

- Colleen is thankful for who she is and what she has. She doesn't brag about things she's good at, or criticize other people.

- Nickolas knows how it feels to disobey God, and he knows how good he feels when he remembers that God forgives him. He forgives others and is kind to them even when they hurt his feelings.

- Paige disobeyed God, and she's heartbroken about it. She knows that sin brings sadness, but asking God's forgiveness brings comfort.

11B © 1994 by The STANDARD PUBLISHING COMPANY. Permission is granted to photocopy this page for ministry purposes only—not for resale.

The Heart of It All

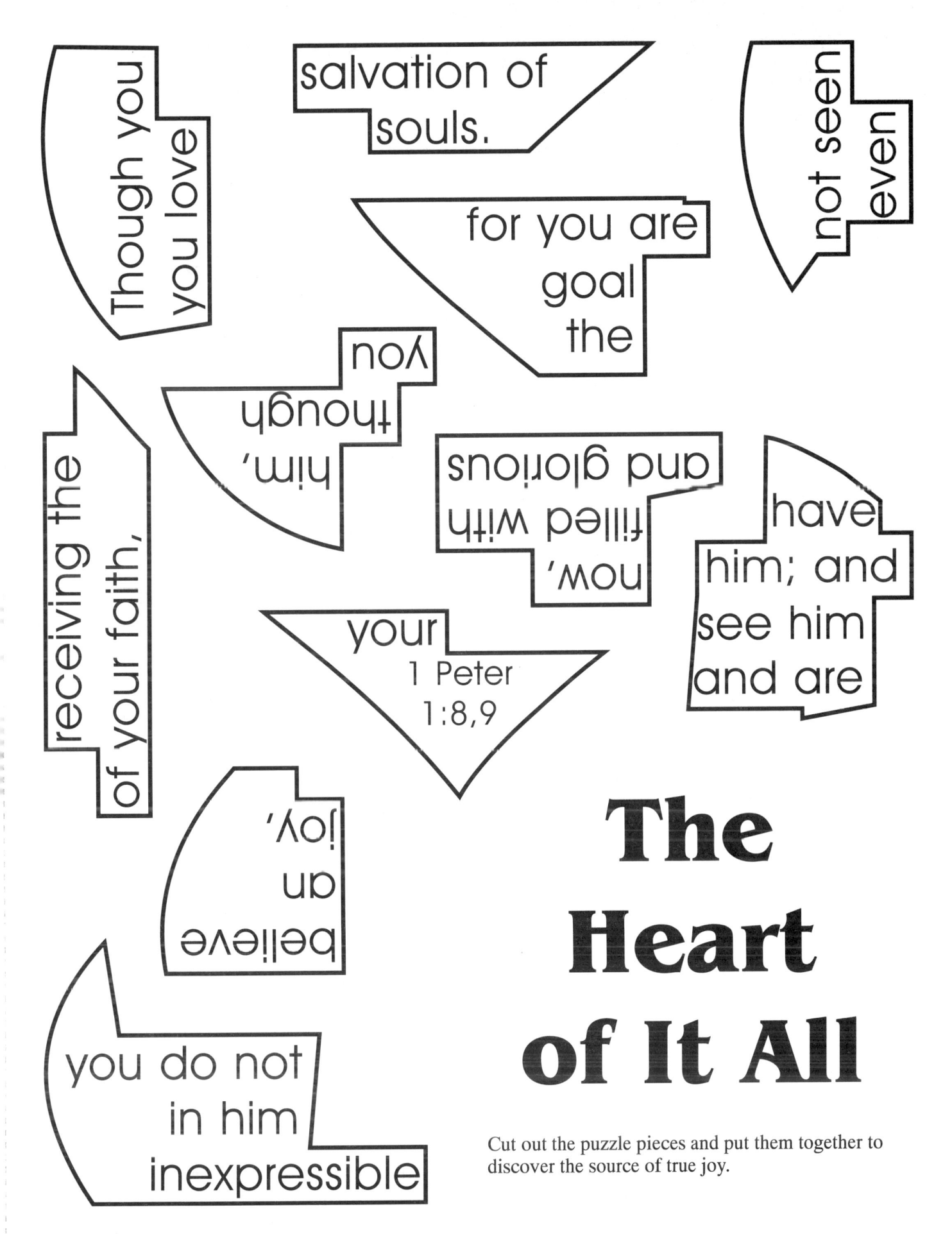

Cut out the puzzle pieces and put them together to discover the source of true joy.

Puzzle pieces (text fragments from 1 Peter 1:8,9):
- Though you
- you love
- salvation of souls.
- not seen even
- for you are goal the
- you though him,
- now, filled with and glorious
- have him; and see him and are
- receiving the of your faith,
- your 1 Peter 1:8,9
- believe an joy,
- you do not in him inexpressible

© 1994 by The STANDARD PUBLISHING COMPANY. Permission is granted to photocopy this page for ministry purposes only—not for resale.

Bible Story: Put Jesus First
Mark 10:17-22

Unit 3: Jesus Teaches About Happiness
Session 12

Worship Focus: Worship God because He is more important than anyone or anything.

More Important Than Anything

Transition Time
10-15 minutes

Allow pupils to go to the rest rooms and to the drinking fountain before they get involved with this activity.

Team Action: For this activity you will need several adult volunteers, copies of Activity Page 12A, and markers. Assign each pupil a team with an adult monitor. Give each pupil a copy of the activity page, which has a list of actions to accomplish. There are more actions on the page than the pupils will be able to accomplish in the allotted time. At a signal, the teams will try to do as many of the actions as they can in the given time. They do not have to do the actions in order. The adult monitor will initial completed actions for each team member. When the time is up, the team with the most actions completed wins.

Launching the Theme
10 minutes

Talk about the transition game. **How did you choose which actions you would do first on your list?** (Pupils respond. Chose actions that were easiest, quickest; knew how to do the actions, and so on.) **Did you finish all the actions on the list?** (No, there was not enough time.)

Each day we have many things to which we could give our attention, but our time is limited. We must choose the things that are most important. God created us. He gave us our lives, our time, the people we love, and everything we own. God is more important than people or things. Today we will worship God because He is more important than anyone or anything.

Briefly explain the choices of preparation for worship. You may allow the pupils to choose the groups in which they would like to participate.

Building the Theme
30 minutes

E easy   **I** independent   **A** advanced

1 Call to Worship **I**
Pupils will research famous people and contrast God's greatness with theirs by writing poems. For this activity you will need to provide articles that would interest your pupils about famous or powerful people, a children's encyclopedia (a good resource for historical figures), Bibles, paper, pencils. If pupils will be working independently, tape or write brief instructions for them.

Have the pupils begin by reading the following Scriptures: Genesis 1:1; Psalms 22:27, 28; and 102:25-27. **What do these verses say about God?** (Allow pupils to respond. God created the heavens and earth. He rules over all people. While other things perish, God will remain the same.) **Make a list of reasons God is more important than anything or anyone.**

Provide a large sheet of paper and a marker. Assign each famous or powerful person, and a resource with which to research that person, to each pupil. Ask the pupils to write two-line poems. The first line will tell why the person is important. The second line will tell why God is more important. When pupils have completed their poems, they will write them on the paper. As a Call to Worship, each pupil will read his poem.

2 Devotion A

Pupils will prepare scenes portraying the story of the rich young ruler to add to the photo album. For this activity, pupils will need copies of Activity Page 12B, the photo album from the past two weeks, an instant camera, Bible costumes and props, pencils, and Bibles.

Label the album pages for today, "God Is More Important Than Anything." Then have pupils read the story of the rich young ruler from Mark 10:17-22. During the session, pupils will do the following: (1) Survey the Scriptures. (2) Decide which scenes to portray. (3) Choose characters and props, pose the scenes, and take the photographs. (4) Mount and label pictures.

During *Sharing in Worship*, pupils will show and explain the pictures in the photo album.

3 Music E

Pupils will praise God in song. For this activity you will need copies of the words and music of the song, "I Exalt Thee," Bibles, several sizes and colors of scarves, and a Bible dictionary. Have a tape of the song, if possible.

Have a pupil look up the meaning of the word *exalt*. **What does "exalt" mean?** (Have the meaning read aloud. "Exalt" means to raise high; to glorify.) Then have the pupils read the following Scriptures together as a class: Psalms 30:1; 34:3; and 99:5. **What do these verses say about exalting? And who are we to exalt?** (Psalm 30:1—Exalt God because He has helped us in trouble. Psalm 34:3—Exalt God's name together. Psalm 99:5—Exalt God because He is holy.) **Is there any other person or anything like Him?** (No.)

Play the song several times as the children listen and learn the words to the song. Then have the pupils practice moving and waving the scarves in the air while the song is being sung. Pupils should be prepared to lead their song after the Devotion, during *Sharing in Worship*. Also choose one pupil to explain the meaning of "exalt," and one or more to read the verses from Psalms.

4 Offering

Pupils will illustrate important items and write praise statements about God. For this activity you will need sugar, water, colored chalk, colored paper, and markers. Before the activity begins, dissolve six tablespoons of sugar in ¼ cup water. Soak chalk 10 minutes.

Give pupils the colored paper. Each pupil will draw a chalk picture of the most important thing he or she owns. Below the picture, the pupil will write a praise sentence telling God why He is more important than the item pictured. **What item do you consider to be the most important thing you own?** (Allow pupils to respond.) **Why is God more important than the item you drew?** (Allow pupils to respond. For example, if a pupil drew a skateboard, he could say, "God created the materials to make the skateboard. He gave me the ability to balance and move so I can ride my skateboard.") During *Sharing in Worship*, pupils will display their chalk pictures and say their praise sentences.

5 Scripture
Pupils will write news bulletins about Bible people who put Jesus first in their lives. Provide copies of Activity Page 12C, Bibles, and pencils.

Pupils will find examples in Scripture of Bible people who put Jesus first. They will write news bulletins and headlines to summarize the events. Divide the group into teams. Have each team choose a Scripture reference and read the account. Each will then write a two- or three-sentence news bulletin that answers the questions on the activity page. Remind pupils that newspaper style is factual—no opinions added. Have pupils think of a headline for each news bulletin. Work together to develop an example similar to this:

Local Fishermen Quit Jobs

SEA OF GALILEE—Two brothers, Peter and Andrew, left their Capernaum fishing business today to follow a teacher named Jesus (Matthew 4:18-20).

During *Sharing in Worship*, pupils will read their news bulletins and headlines.

6 Praise Prayer
Pupils will write and tape record sentence prayers about the importance of God. You will need to provide paper, a blank cassette tape, tape recorder, and pencils.

Ask each pupil to finish this sentence: "God, You are more important than _____." Make a list of what the pupils say. These sentences will form a prayer of praise. When the pupils are ready, ask each one to record his prayer sentence on the cassette. Encourage each pupil to participate.

Some pupils may prefer to write their sentences first and read them into the recorder. Use the pause button between each pupil's recording so no one feels rushed. When the pupils have finished the recorded prayer, rewind the tape and play it back so the pupils can listen to their prayer. Pupils will share their prayer of praise with the rest of the group at the end of *Sharing in Worship*.

Sharing in Worship
20-25 minutes

If you did not have pupils do all the activities, plan to present them yourself or have another adult or two help you. Omit any activity that is too involved for you to do without help from the group.

Call to Worship
Group 1 has researched some very famous and important people. Have pupils, one at a time, recite their poems. **Today, we are worshiping God because He is more important than anything or anyone.**

Devotion
Group 2 has prepared scenes portraying the story of the rich young ruler, found in Mark 10:17-22. Have the members of Group 2 share their information from the photo album.

The rich young ruler had a favorite possession. What was his favorite possession? (Money.) **Was he willing to give it up for God?** (No.) **Why not?** (Because, to him it was more important than God was.)

The young man had studied the Scriptures and had known the commandments since he was a boy. Wasn't that enough? (No.) **God knew that money and possessions took first place in the young man's life. God asks all of us to love Him more than we love our money or anything or anyone.**

Music

Have a member of Group 3 explain the meaning of the word *exalt*. Have another member read Psalms 30:1; 34:3; and 99:5. Then have Group 3 lead the song, "I Exalt Thee," singing it through once. Then have the group lead the song again as they move and wave their scarves in the air.

Lord's Supper

One reason God is more important than anything or anyone is because He gave His Son to die for our sins. Jesus was the only sacrifice good enough to pay for the sins of the whole world! And God is the only one who could raise His Son from the dead. Let's think about Jesus' suffering and death right now and praise God for the gift of eternal life through Jesus.

Offering

Sing a praise song before having the children take up the offering. **Along with praise sentences to God, Group 2 has created chalk pictures of the most important things they own.** Allow one pupil at a time to show his or her chalk picture and say a praise sentence. **We are showing God that He is more important than anyone or anything right now by giving our offerings to Him. Because God is the most important person to us, we can give money back to Him knowing He will take care of our every need. God is certain. God is true.**

Scripture

Pass out copies of Activity Page 12C.

Group 5 has written some headlines and news bulletins to summarize stories of Bible people who put Jesus first. Have members of Group 5 read their headlines and news bulletins.

Praise Prayer

Have Group 6 present their prayers of praise. **We have worshiped God today because He is more important than anyone or anything.**

After pupils from Group 6 play the recording of their prayer, form a circle and let volunteers pray sentence prayers.

Closing Moments

10-15 minutes

"Seek Ye First" Game. Before beginning this activity, on the floor mark an 8' square; then divide this into four equal squares, using tape or colored chalk. Have the pupils read Matthew 6:33 together as a class. Then have a pupil stand in each of the four squares. Give one of the pupils a big ball. Tell the pupil to bounce the ball in another square. The pupil in that square will catch the ball, letting the ball bounce only once. Then that pupil will bounce the ball in another square. Continue repeating this procedure until someone misses a ball or there is more than one bounce inside a square. The person who misses the ball or lets it bounce more than once, must recite Matthew 6:33. Make this a game of fun, not competition.

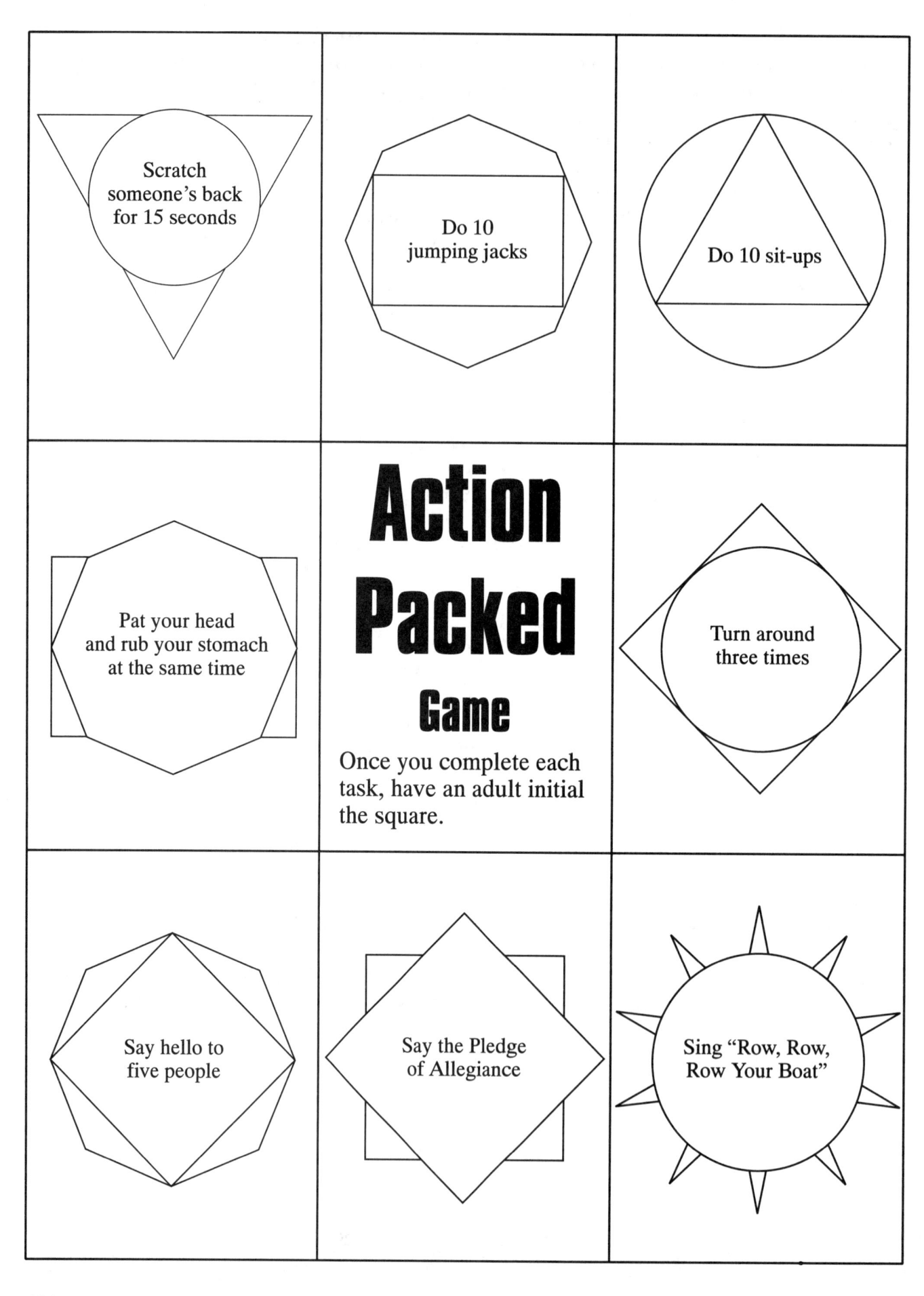

Scratch someone's back for 15 seconds	Do 10 jumping jacks	Do 10 sit-ups
Pat your head and rub your stomach at the same time	**Action Packed Game** — Once you complete each task, have an adult initial the square.	Turn around three times
Say hello to five people	Say the Pledge of Allegiance	Sing "Row, Row, Row Your Boat"

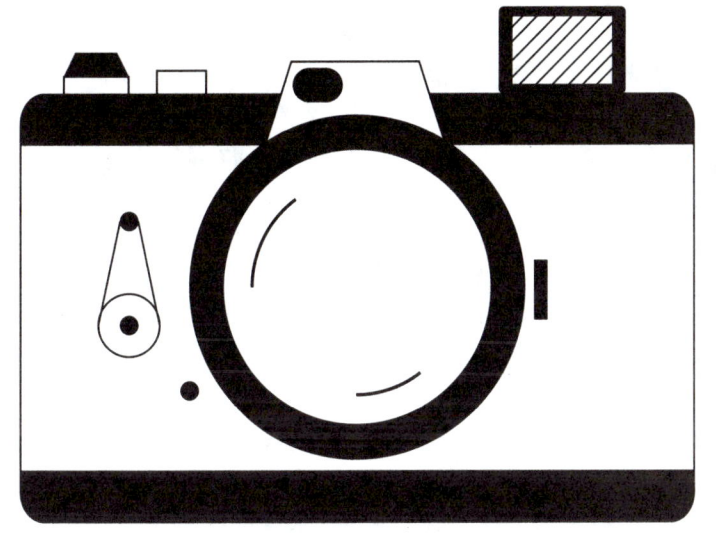

Photos for an Album

Read the Scripture. Mark phrases as you read that you may want to use for your photo album.

Label the pages **God Is More Important Than Anything.** Then plan and pose scenes to illustrate the Bible story, photograph them and mount the photos in the album.

Ideas for scenes:

_____

_____

_____

_____

_____

_____

_____

Mark 10:17-22

As Jesus started on his way, a man ran up to him and fell on his knees before him. "Good teacher," he asked, "what must I do to inherit eternal life?"

"Why do you call me good?" Jesus answered. "No one is good—except God alone. You know the commandments: 'Do not murder, do not commit adultery, do not steal, do not give false testimony, do not defraud, honor your father and mother.'"

"Teacher," he declared, "all these I have kept since I was a boy."

Jesus looked at him and loved him. "One thing you lack," he said. "Go, sell everything you have and give to the poor, and you will have treasure in heaven. Then come, follow me."

At this the man's face fell. He went away sad, because he had great wealth.

© 1994 by The STANDARD PUBLISHING COMPANY. Permission is granted to photocopy this page for ministry purposes only—not for resale.

Write the News

Read the Scripture to find out about people who put Jesus first. Then write a news bulletin to summarize the events. One has been done for you. Remember to include answers to the questions, Who? What? When? Where? Why? One has been done for you.

Matthew 4:18-20-Local Fishermen Quit Jobs
Sea of Galilee-Two brothers, Peter and Andrew, left their Capernaum fishing business today to follow a teacher named Jesus.

Matthew 4:12, 13, 21, 22

Matthew 9:9

John 1:43-49

Luke 10:38-42

Luke 19:1-10

Mark 14:3-9

Bible Story: How to Build a Happy Life
Matthew 7:24-29

Unit 3: Jesus Teaches About Happiness
Session 13

Worship Focus: Worship God because His Word will last forever.

For Eternity

Transition Time
10-15 minutes

Send the children in small groups to the rest rooms and drinking fountain. Welcome newcomers and involve everyone in the following activity.

Building Blocks Relay. For this activity you will need several sets of small building blocks or dominoes. Line up the group in two or more teams at the opposite end of the room from each set of blocks. At the starting signal, pupils must run to the blocks, add one block to the stack, and run back to tag the next team member. All team members must place one block on the stack. The first team to have every member place a block on the stack, without its falling, wins. If a block falls, the team must start over. Play again, asking each team member to add one block to make a shape, such as a circle.

Launching the Theme
10 minutes

Have ready several advice columns, articles about music groups, and advertisements for clothing or games that interest your pupils. Display the articles where pupils can see them easily.

The block towers and circles you built didn't last long. They could be knocked down or rearranged very quickly. Much of what we consider important in our world will not last either. These articles talk about things that are important to you and important to our society right now. But twenty-five years from now, these music groups probably won't be popular. These clothes will be outdated, and the games may no longer be available. And this advice will be replaced by new, "updated" advice. These articles will become historical memorabilia that remind us what things were like twenty-five years earlier.

God's Word contains many historical events. They help us understand what the world was like many years ago. But God's Word is more than just a history book. God's Word also contains advice that will never be outdated. God's Word is always true. Today we will worship God because His Word will last forever.

Briefly explain the choices of preparation for worship. You may allow the pupils to choose the groups in which they would like to participate.

Building the Theme
30 minutes

E easy **I** independent **A** advanced

1 Call to Worship E

Pupils will contrast worldly items with God's eternal Word. For this activity you will need to provide articles from *Launching the Theme*, large pieces of coarse sandpaper, crayons, foil, cookie sheets, a toaster oven, and Bibles.

Pupils will choose pictures of objects from the articles or draw their own objects to illustrate things that will not last. Instruct the pupils to draw their pictures on the sandpaper by pressing down hard with the crayons. Bake the pictures on a foil-covered cookie sheet for 10-15 seconds in a 250° oven.

Let's read 1 Peter 1:25. (Do so at this time.) **What does this verse say to you?** (Allow pupils to respond.) **Write a paraphrase of 1 Peter 1:25 on your illustrations.**

During *Sharing in Worship*, each pupil will say why or how his or her object or item will not last. Then the whole group will repeat the paraphrase. (For example, one pupil could say, "Nike® tennis shoes will wear out and someday will not be made anymore." The entire group would then say, "But God's Word lasts forever.") Practice presenting the pictures and saying the praise statement together.

2 Special Music

Pupils will prepare to present a "song and light" show. They will need copies of the words and a tape of the song, "Thy Word Is a Lamp Unto My Feet," flashlights, several colors of lightbulbs, and Bibles. Pupils will sing through the song several times, then create a light show, using their flashlights, while the song is being played.

Singing is one way we can praise God because His Word will last forever. Let's read Psalm 119:105. (Allow a volunteer to read the verse.) **What is like a lamp unto our feet?** (God's Word.) **What else does God's Word light besides our feet?** (Our path.) **Today we are going to practice this song with a light show to present during our worship time.** Decide what colors of light to use and how to use the lights during the song. Then, in a darkened corner of the room, or in another room, practice using the flashlights with the song. The pupils will present their light show immediately after the Call to Worship.

3 Scripture

By completing the activity page, pupils will learn that God's Word will last forever. For this activity you will need copies of Activity Page 13A, Bibles, and pencils.

Pass out copies of the activity page and have pupils complete the activity. Then focus a discussion on God's Word. **Will everything on earth last forever?** (No.) **What will last forever?** (God's Word.) **What do these Scriptures say about God's Word.** (Allow pupils to respond. Psalms 119:89—stands firm; 119:144—forever right; 119:160—true, eternal; Proverbs 30:5—flawless, a shield to us; Isaiah 40:8—stands forever; Matthew 24:35—will never pass away.) **We can worship God because His Word will last forever.** The message will be decoded during *Sharing in Worship*.

4 Devotion A

Pupils will prepare scenes portraying the story of the wise and foolish builders. Pupils will need copies of Activity Page 13B, photo album from the past three weeks, an instant camera, Bible costumes and props, pencils, and Bibles.

Label the album pages for today, "God's Word Lasts Forever." Then have pupils pose scenes for the story of the wise and foolish builders, from Matthew 7:24-27. During the activity, pupils will do the following: (1) Survey the Scriptures. (2) Decide which scenes to portray. (3) Choose characters and props, pose the scene, and take the photographs. (4) Mount and label pictures in the album.

During *Sharing in Worship*, pupils will share the information from the photo album.

5 Music [E]

Pupils will write words for a song about God's Word. Provide a large tablet of paper on an easel or a large piece of paper tacked to the wall, copies of the words and music to "God Is So Good," Bibles, paper, markers, and pencils. A tape of the song will be helpful.

Ask pupils to read the following Scriptures: Psalm 119:89, 105, 144, 160; Proverbs 30:5; Isaiah 40:8; Matthew 24:35; John 17:17. **List things the Scriptures tell us about God's Word.** (Allow pupils to respond while one of the pupils writes the list on a piece of paper.) Let pupils listen to and/or sing "God Is So Good." **Using the words from this list, write words to this melody.** Help the pupils write several stanzas to the song. (For example: "God's Word is true. God's Word is true. God's Word is true, It's so true for me.") Ask a pupil to print the words on the song chart and let others illustrate the chart appropriately. Practice singing the song several times. During *Sharing in Worship*, display the chart as the pupils lead the large group in singing the song.

6 Personal Prayer [I]

Pupils will create sand pictures in jars after reading Matthew 24:35. You will need white sand, food coloring, shaker jars, paper towels, clean and dry baby food jars and lids, and Bibles.

Ahead of time, dye the sand by placing white sand and food coloring in a jar. Shake the sand until it is evenly dyed. Spread it out on paper toweling and allow it to dry before using. Place each color in a jar, preferably with a shaker top. If you do not have time to make the colored sand, check with your local craft store to purchase some. Or, if you prefer, choose another art medium to use.

Begin the activity by saying, **Let's read Matthew 24:35.** (Have the class say the verse together until everyone can recite the verse without looking.) **What things will pass away or disappear?** (Heaven and earth.) **If those things pass away, will anything remain? If so, what?** (Word of God.) **How long will the Word of God last?** (Forever.) Instruct pupils how to add layers of colored sand to their jars. Designs can be created by varying the thickness of these layers. During *Sharing in Worship*, the pupils will display their sand pictures while they recite Matthew 24:35. Have several pupils prepared to end with sentence prayers.

Sharing in Worship

20-25 minutes

If you did not have pupils do all the activities, plan to present them yourself or have another adult or two help you. Omit any activity that is too involved for you to do without help from the group.

Call to Worship

Group 1 has drawn objects to illustrate things that will not last. Have each member display and tell why his or her object will not last. Then have the group say their paraphrase of 1 Peter 1:25.

Music

Group 2 has prepared a special musical light show for us. Have a member of Group 2 read Psalm 119:105. Then have the group perform their light show during the song, "Thy Word Is a Lamp Unto My Feet."

Lord's Supper

Just as God's Word is everlasting, so is His love for us. When Jesus took the punishment for our sins, He bought for us the opportunity to enjoy God's love forever.

Scripture

Group 3 has discovered a secret message about the Word of God. Have Group 3 relay their message to the class. Have the rest of the class decode the message on Activity Page 13A.

Devotion
Group 4 has prepared scenes portraying the story of the wise and foolish builders found in Matthew 7:24-27. Have members of Group 4 share their information from the photo album.

Today's story tells us that, if we ignore Jesus and do whatever we like, we may have a good time for a while. But when troubles come, our pleasant lives will fall apart. It may seem to be easier to do as we please, instead of reading the Bible and finding what Jesus wants us to do, but this is foolish.

If we find a happy life by reading and doing God's Word, our happiness lasts through all our troubles. We can be happy even when it seems that everyone is against us. But we cannot be happy unless we keep doing what God's Word tells us to do.

Offering
One way we can praise God because His Word will last forever, is by giving back part of what the Lord has given to us. Our offerings can help tell others that God's Word is forever.

Devotion
Group 5 has made a song chart to use with the song, "God Is So Good." Have members of Group 5 display their song chart as they lead the class in singing the new words to the song.

Personal Praise
Group 6 has created sand pictures and can recite a very important verse for us. Have members display their sand pictures while they recite Matthew 24:35. Then have members lead the class in memorizing the verse. Have everyone come together in a prayer circle. **As we have our prayer time, let's praise God because His Word will last forever.** Have volunteers (or designated pupils) pray aloud.

Closing Moments
10-15 minutes

Praise Postcards. Pupils will send postcards to friends, using sentences praising God because His Word will last forever. They will need old greeting cards, rulers, black markers, postage stamps for postcards, phone book or church directory, and Bibles.

Have each pupil cut the picture side of a greeting card from the back of the card. (Set aside the back of the card.) Then, place the card horizontally with the picture side down, and draw a thick black line down the middle of the card. On the left side, write a sentence to a friend or family member, praising God for the things the Bible says about His Word. On the right side of the card, write that person's name and address. Place a postage stamp in the upper right-hand corner of the card. Collect the postcards and mail them during the week.

Match the Shape

Fill in the blanks by matching the shape of the missing word to the words in the list. You will discover some important facts about God's Word. If you need help, look up the verses in the Bible. Several words are used more than once.

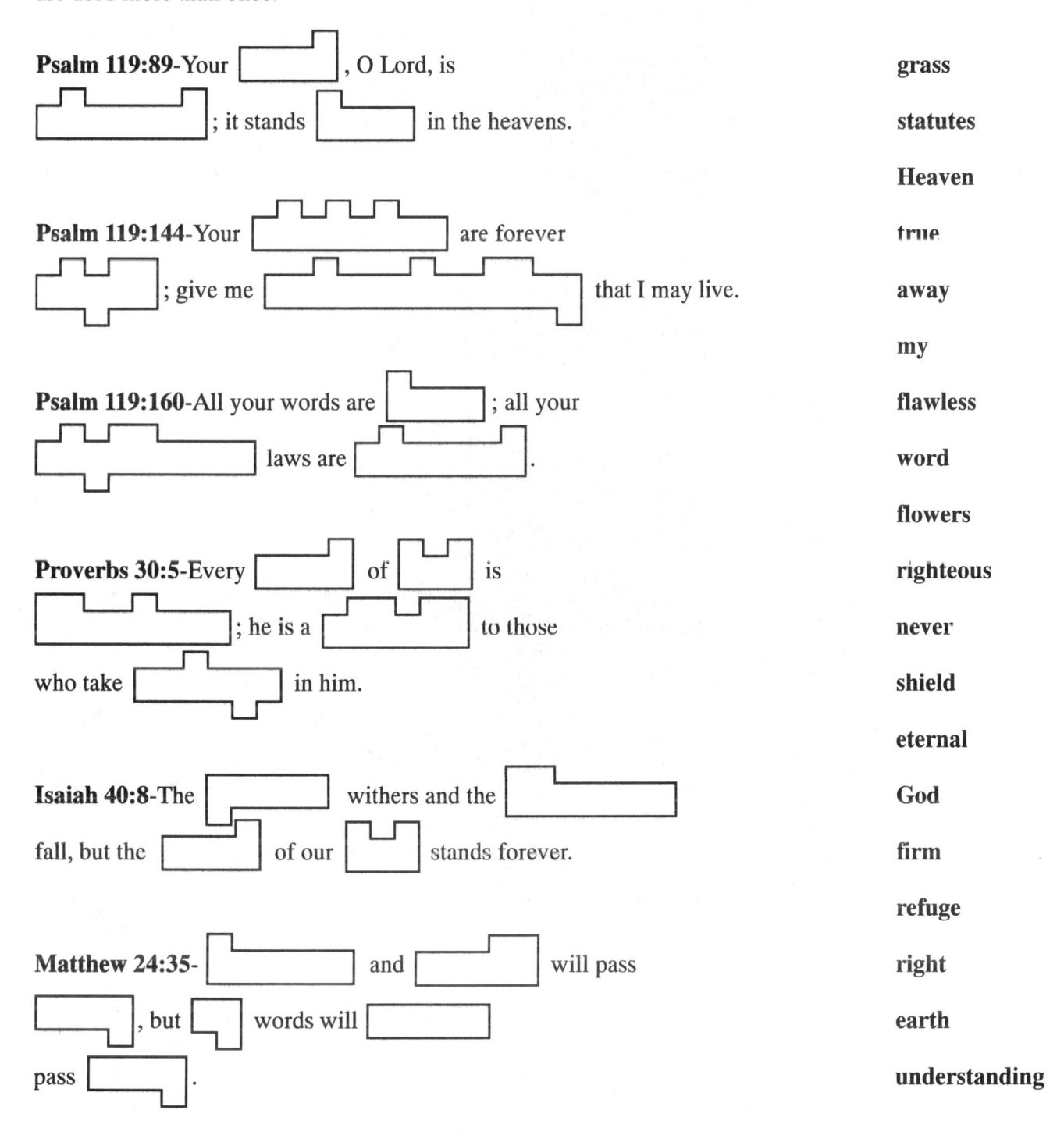

Psalm 119:89-Your _____, O Lord, is _____; it stands _____ in the heavens.

Psalm 119:144-Your _____ are forever _____; give me _____ that I may live.

Psalm 119:160-All your words are _____; all your _____ laws are _____.

Proverbs 30:5-Every _____ of _____ is _____; he is a _____ to those who take _____ in him.

Isaiah 40:8-The _____ withers and the _____ fall, but the _____ of our _____ stands forever.

Matthew 24:35-_____ and _____ will pass _____, but _____ words will _____ pass _____.

grass
statutes
Heaven
true
away
my
flawless
word
flowers
righteous
never
shield
eternal
God
firm
refuge
right
earth
understanding

A Lesson in Construction

Read Matthew 7:24-29. Use the squares below to sketch out scenes to illustrate the parable. Using costumes and props, pose the scenes and photograph them for your photo album.

13B   © 1994 by The STANDARD PUBLISHING COMPANY. Permission is granted to photocopy this page for ministry purposes only—not for resale.